INDIANS OF NORTH AMERICA

THIS BOOK BELONGS TO:

K. MAHONEY

HEINEMANN
EDUCATIONAL

Fiona Reynoldson
Paul Shuter

Heinemann Educational,
a division of Heinemann Educational Books Ltd,
Halley Court, Jordan Hill, Oxford OX2 8EJ

OXFORD LONDON EDINBURGH MADRID
ATHENS BOLOGNA PARIS MELBOURNE
SYDNEY AUCKLAND SINGAPORE TOKYO
IBADAN NAIROBI HARARE GABORONE
PORTSMOUTH NH (USA)

First published 1992

93 94 95 96 97 10 9 8 7 6 5 4 3

**British Library Cataloguing in Publication Data is available
from the British Library on request.**

ISBN 0-435-31426-2

Designed by Ron Kamen, Green Door Design Ltd, Basingstoke

Illustrated by Phill Burrows and Jeff Edwards

Printed in Spain by Mateu Cromo

The front cover shows 'Leader of the Mandan Buffalo Bull
Society'.

Icon information

Every Unit in this book includes the following symbol. When
a section is filled in, it indicates the availability of extra
resources included in the accompanying *Assessment and
Resources Pack*.

Unit is referred to
in an Extension
Worksheet.

Unit is referred to
in an Assessment Exercise.

For every Unit there is a Foundation Worksheet.

Acknowledgements

The authors and publishers would like to thank Professor
Christine Bolt of the University of Kent for her comments on the
original manuscript.
The authors and publishers would like to thank the following for
permission to reproduce photographs:

British Museum: 2.1A, 2.2A, 2.2C, 2.3A, 2.3E, 2.4B, 2.4F
Werner Forman Archive: 1.1A
Glenbow Museum, Canada: 3.4B
Joslyn Art Museum, Omaha, Nebraska: 1.1B, 4.1D
David Muench © 1992: 1.4A, 1.4B
National Archives of Canada, Ottawa: 3.11A, 3.11E
© National Geographic Society, Richard Schlecht: 3.7A
New York Public Library, Rare Books and Manuscripts Division,
Astor, Lennox and Tilden Foundations: 3.5A
Peter Newark's Western Americana: 3.2B, 3.7D, 3.10D, 3.12D,
3.13D, 4.1A, 4.2B, 4.3C, 4.5C, 4.7B, 4.7 bottom middle, 4.8A
NHPA/Brian Hawkes: 2.1 middle right
Oxford Scientific Films © Tom Ulrich: 4.2, top p.51
Royal Ontario Museum: 3.6C, 3.8C
Salamander Books Ltd: 3.3A, 3.4A, 3.11F
Scott T. Smith: 3.1A
Smithsonian Institution: 3.8B, 3.13B, 4.4A
Southwest Museum, Los Angeles: 4.7C
University of California, Bancroft Library: 3.3D, 3.6D
University of Colorado Museum (photo by Joe Ben Wheat): 1.1
bottom right

Reprinted from 'A Pictographic History of the Oglala Sioux' by
Amos Bad Heart Bull, text by Helen H. Glish, by permission of
University of Nebraska Press. Copyright © 1967 by the University
of Nebraska Press: 4.2C, 4.2H, 4.3A, 4.3D, 4.4D, 4.5A, 4.5B, 4.5F,
4.6F, 4.6C, 4.6D, 4.6E, 4.8C
Washington State University: 3.1D
Yale University, Beinecke Rare Book and Manuscript Library: 3.10A
Every effort has been made to contact copyright holders of material
reproduced in this book. Any omissions will be rectified in
subsequent printings if notice is given to the publisher.

Details of Written Sources
In some sources the wording or sentence structure has been
simplified to ensure that the source is accessible.

Michael Alexander (Ed.), *Discovering the New World: Based on the
Works of Theodore de Bry*, Harper and Row, 1976: 2.2B, 2.3B, 2.3C,
2.3D, 2.4A, 2.4A, C and E
Le Roy H. Appleton, *American Indian Design and Decoration*, Dover
Publications, 1971: 3.5C, 3.6A
Luther Standing Bear, *Land of the Spotted Eagle*, Boston, 1933: 4.2F,
4.4C
Dr F. Boas, *The Kwakiutl of Vancouver Island*, American Museum of
Natural History, 1985: 3.9A
W. Brandon, *The American Heritage Book of the Indians*, American
Heritage Publishing Company, 1961: 3.11B
Dee Brown, *Bury My Heart at Wounded Knee*, Holt, Rinehart &
Winston, 1971: 4.8B
George Catlin, *Letters and Notes: Manners, Customs and Conditions
of the North American Indians*, New York, 1844: 4.4F
Robert Claiborne, *The First Americans*, Times Incorporated, 1973:
3.2A, 3.10C
T. Crosby, *Up and Down the North Pacific Coast by Canoe and Mission
Ship*, Toronto, 1914: 3.8A
Richard Irving Dodge, *The Hunting Grounds of the Great West*, 1877:
4.1B
Philip Drucker, *Indians of the North West Coast*, McGraw Hill, 1955:
3.3B, 3.10B
Chief William Red Fox, *The Memoirs of Chief Red Fox*, W.H. Allen,
1971: 4.3E
Horace Greeley, *An Overland Journey from New York to San Francisco
in the Summer of 1859*, 1895: 1.1C
D. Jenness, *The Indians of Canada*, National Museum of Canada,
Anthropological Series 15, 1932: 3.2D, 3.3C, 3.4D
Aldona Jonaitis, *Art of the Northern Tlingit*, University of
Washington Press, 1989: 3.2C, 3.6B
Philip Kopper, *The Smithsonian Book of North American Indians before
the Coming of the Europeans*, Smithsonian Books, 1986: 1.2B
Aurel Krause, *The Tlingit Indians – Results of a Trip to the North West
Coast of America and the Bering Straits in 1881*, University of
Washington Press, 1956: 3.1B, 3.4B, 3.4C, 3.7C, 3.11D, 3.12C, 3.13A
Sir Alexander Mackenzie, *Voyages from Montreal on the River St.
Lawrence Through the Continent of North America in 1789 and 1793*,
London, 1801: 3.12A
J. Neihardt, *Black Elk Speaks*, Sphere, 1974: 4.4B, 4.4E, 4.5E
Francis Parkman, *The Oregon Trail*, 1847: 4.1E, 4.2A, 4.2D, 4.3B,
4.6A, 4.6B
Maria Parker Pascua, 'Ozette', *National Geographic Magazine*, October
1991: 3.1C
Helen Peterson, 'Ozette', *National Geographic Magazine*, October
1991: 3.5B
Alexander Ross, *Adventures on the Columbia River*, London, 1849: 3.7B
Schools Council Project: History 13–16, *The American West
1840–95*, Holmes McDougall, 1977: 4.1C
George Simpson, *Narrative of a Journey Round the World during the
Years 1841–2*, London, 1847: 3.12B
Matthew W. Stirling, *Indians of the Americas*, National Geographic
Society, 1955: 3.9B
Frederick W. Turner III (Ed.), *The Portable North American Indian
Reader*, Viking, 1973: 3.7E, 3.13C
Anthony Wallace, *The Death and Rebirth of the Seneca*, 1970: 2.1B
Wilcomb E. Washburn, *The Indian in America*, Harper and Row,
1975: 2.1C, 4.2G

CONTENTS

1.1 The Evidence

In this book you will study the people who lived in North America before the first Europeans arrived there. This is not easy. The name we usually use to describe these people – **Indians** – shows one of the problems. Christopher Columbus first called them Indians because he thought he had landed in or near India. He was completely wrong. He didn't understand the language of the people he met, so he couldn't learn from them that he was nowhere near India. However, much of our information about the Indians comes from people like Columbus: Europeans or their descendants who didn't always understand the people they met.

The Indians themselves had no written languages, so the tales of the travellers and settlers cannot be corrected by the Indians' own accounts. This is a problem. Without written evidence from the Indians themselves it is hard to understand the life of Indian groups either before or after White settlement changed their world.

Historians have many other sources to use. Archaeologists have discovered much about many Indian tribes. **Artifacts** survive from many places. From this evidence it is often possible to work out what happened, or how people lived. But why they did things and what they thought is much harder to discover. Usually we rely on language to tell one another these things, but written evidence about the Indians often comes from hostile witnesses.

Whites who created sources about the Indians and their way of life had their own motives. Often they wanted to justify their treatment of the Indians as they pushed them from their lands and herded them on to reservations. Sometimes they wanted to praise the Indians. Some 19th century archaeologists wanted to show that America had as glamorous a past as Europe had.

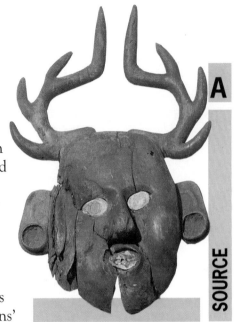

A SOURCE

A mask carved by Indians in what is now Oklahoma before they had any contact with Whites.

B SOURCE

A buffalo skull perched on rocks, seen and painted by Karl Bodmer, a Swiss artist on an expedition up the Missouri River in the 1830s.

The Indians are children. Their wars, treaties, habitations, crafts, comforts, all belong to the very lowest ages of human existence. Proud and worthless, lazy and lousy, they will strut or drink out their miserable existence, and at length give the world relief by dying out of it.

Horace Greeley, an American politician, in a book, 'An Overland Journey from New York to San Francisco in the Summer of 1859', 1859.

Activities...

1 North American Indians left no written records before they came into contact with Whites. Why does this make things hard for historians?

2 a What can you learn from Source A?

   b Historians have suggested that **shamans** (medicine men) wore the mask for dancing to bring good luck for their hunters. Is this fact or opinion?

   c The artist said Source B was a magical device made by hunters to attract buffalo. Is this fact or opinion?

3 Read Source C. Do you think Greeley is likely to be a reliable witness?

4 Explain the evidence you think Joe Ben Wheat used to back up each of his conclusions (a–h).

A buffalo hunt 8,500 years ago

Prehistoric Indians hunted buffalo by driving them over cliffs so they were killed by the fall. Buffalo moved in herds and had their young in late spring. They had a very good sense of smell, but very poor eyesight. If a herd was stampeded the animals in front wouldn't see a cliff until it was too late to stop. Those charging behind would force them over the edge. The American archaeologist Joe Ben Wheat studied the remains of such a hunt. This is what he found:

- the remains of nearly 200 buffalo in a dry gulley running east to west
- 16 of the buffalo were calves only a few days old
- none of the animals faced north
- the bones were in three distinct layers
- the animals in the bottom layer had not been cut up at all
- there were lance points in the left sides of some of the animals in the bottom layer
- piles of bones showed where animals had been cut up
- front legs were always at the bottom of these piles of bones
- the small tongue bones [hyoids] were found all over the site and at all levels of the piles of butchered bones
- rib bones were broken on the butchered animals
- the small neck bones [vertebrae] were draped over the front of the skulls.

From this evidence Joe Ben Wheat concluded:

a The hunt took place in early summer.

b The wind was blowing from south to north on the day of the kill.

c The Indians stampeded the buffalo from the north, driving them south.

d Some Indians were waiting to the east of the buffalo to stop them escaping that way.

e The Indians could not get to the animals on the bottom layer because they were wedged too tightly below the others.

f The buffalo's front legs were stripped of meat and removed from the carcass first.

g Early in the butchering the Indians removed the buffalos' tongues, which they ate raw as they carried on with their work.

h The Indians took the internal organs of the buffalo, and last of all the neck meat.

Wheat calculated that the Indians took 25, 692 kg of meat and 5 tonnes of organs and fat from the kill. This was enough to last a band of about 150 Indians for a month.

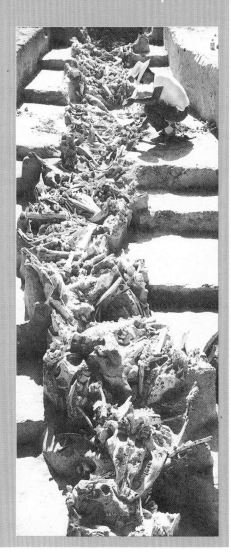

The site of the kill during Wheat's archaeological dig.

1.2 The First Americans

Modern humans – Homo sapiens – first appeared in Africa. In the last 2 million years we have spread throughout the world. By about 10,000 years ago we were living in all the modern continents. When and how did the first humans get to America, a continent which is separated from the rest of the world by two great oceans?

The Ice Age is a key part of the answer to both questions. During the last Ice Age so much water was frozen into glaciers that the sea level dropped by about 140 m. This meant that Alaska (on the northern tip of North America) was joined by land to Asia, over what is now the Bering Sea. Historians call this lost land **Beringia**. It existed for thousands of years before the sea level rose and swallowed it up. So the answer to how humans first got to America is simple – they walked.

It is a mistake to think that groups of early people meant to cross Beringia to get to America. The groups were **nomads** who got their food by hunting animals and gathering plants and fruits. Slowly, over hundreds of generations, more and more people migrated to North and then South America.

The great Laurentide and Cordilleran glaciers separated Beringia and Alaska from the rest of America. Historians are agreed that there was a gap between the two glaciers, which became the main route south. Some historians claim there was a second route, west of the Cordilleran glacier and down the coast.

B SOURCE

Unmistakable signs of ancient human occupation have been found; people used Fell's Cave in Chile about 11,000 years ago.

From 'North American Indians before the Coming of the European' by Philip Kopper, 1986.

A graph from the 'Times Atlas of Modern History'. It shows changes in temperature and the rise of human population over the last 100 million years. This graph uses a special type of scale. The further you go back from the present (the right-hand end of the graph), the less space is used. The graph gives the same space to the last 100 years as it does to the previous 1,000, then the same space again for the 10,000 years before that, and so on.

A SOURCE

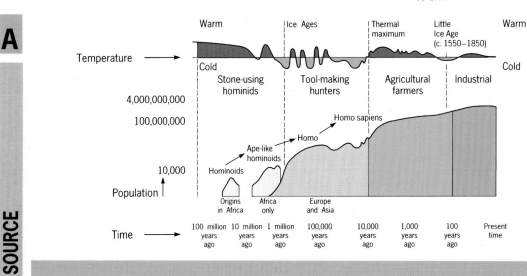

By 11,000 years ago both North and South America were settled by people we now call Indians. There were many different Indian peoples, each with its own culture. They settled the two continents which stretch from near the South Pole to near the North Pole. There are many types of landscape and climate; different cultures developed to match the differences of land and climate. In the area covered by modern California, for instance, people spoke more different languages than in the whole of Europe. Many of these groups left remains from their prehistoric past. When the early European settlers found the remains of these prehistoric peoples they were puzzled. They were unwilling to believe that the Indians were as sophisticated or powerful as the remains suggested.

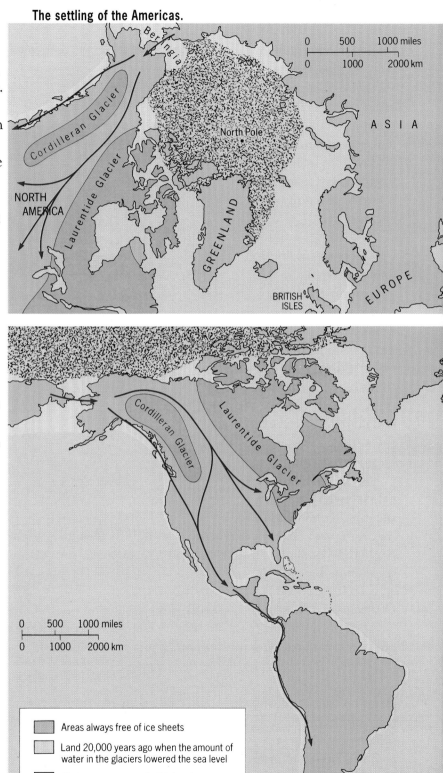

The settling of the Americas.

Areas always free of ice sheets

Land 20,000 years ago when the amount of water in the glaciers lowered the sea level

Glaciers, up to one mile thick in the centre. People could not live on them

Ice cap

Route of people's advance

Activities...

1 a Copy the graph in Source A.
  b Mark on your copy the point at which you think people first settled in America.
  c Explain your reasons for your choice.

2 Why is the date of the remains at Fell's Cave seen as so important in dating the first settlement of America?

3 There were many different Indian cultures in North America. California had more different cultures closer together than any other area. Can you suggest why?

1.3 Language and Environment

Many different Indian cultures grew up in America. Historians have often tried to classify them into types. This makes comparison easier. It also helps historians work out the relationship between different tribes and nations.

The most useful division may be into different **environments**. Some historians have developed a classification based on geology, climate, and plant and animal life. All tribes living within one of these areas would face the same conditions and have the same sorts of opportunities and problems. In some ways this is obvious. Indians in the Arctic region could hardly depend on gathering acorns for their food supply, nor could the woodland tribes of the north east depend on hunting sea mammals.

Environment did not decide everything about the way Indians lived. Within each of these areas there were a variety of ways of life. Some Indians were warlike and others more peaceable, some were nomads and some settled farmers.

Another way of classifying Indian tribes is by the **languages** they spoke. Linguists believe that over 200 different languages were spoken in North America before the first Europeans arrived. These languages can be divided into groups of languages with close links. All these languages were quite different. Speakers of two languages within the same group would be speaking languages as different as French is from Spanish or Italian.

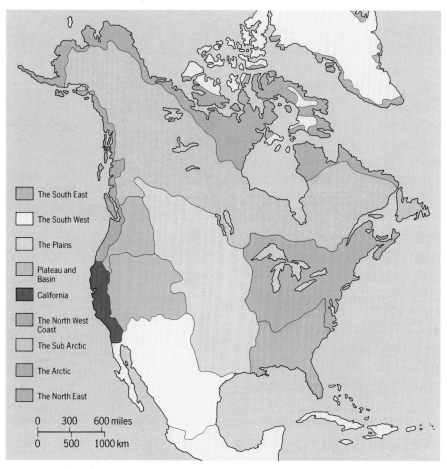

Indian cultures divided into environments.

The South East
The South West
The Plains
Plateau and Basin
California
The North West Coast
The Sub Arctic
The Arctic
The North East

| 0 | 300 | 600 miles |
| 0 | 500 | 1000 km |

The South East Fairly flat lands covered by evergreen forests. High rainfall.

The South West Mountainous, with some areas of desert and some prairie grassland. Low rainfall.

The Plains Largely flat, with a mixture of plains (short) and prairie (taller) grassland. Low rainfall.

Plateau and Basin Forested mountains to the north and land more like the plains to the south.

California Fertile coastal area divided from the rest of America by mountain ranges and deserts.

The North West Coast Mainly coastal with high rainfall and a mild climate.

The Sub Arctic Harsh climate, very cold in winter, with open woodland and tundra.

The Arctic North of the treeline, permafrost.

The North East Deciduous and evergreen forests. High rainfall.

This unit completes the introduction to this study of the Indian peoples of North America. As you have seen, there are two big problems to overcome. How can we find out about the Indian cultures from inside, rather than seeing them through the eyes of outside observers, many of whom were hostile? And should we generalize about such a diverse group of peoples?

The rest of this book uses a **case study** approach. It concentrates on different groups and regions selected to show something of the variety of Indian lifestyles. It also looks at the effect that contact with the European settlers had on those groups. The main case studies are about the Plains Indians and the Indians of the North West Coast. Just to underline the cultural variety, though, the last unit of this part of the book concentrates on a very different culture – the Pueblo Indians of the South West.

North American Indian language groups.

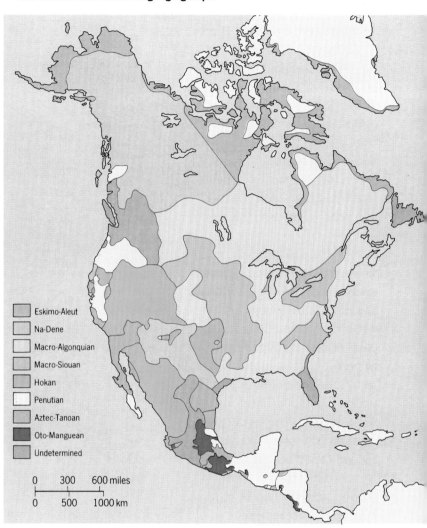

- Eskimo-Aleut
- Na-Dene
- Macro-Algonquian
- Macro-Siouan
- Hokan
- Penutian
- Aztec-Tanoan
- Oto-Manguean
- Undetermined

```
0        300      600 miles
0        500      1000 km
```

Activities...

1 Write out the sentences below, putting the correct heads and tails together.

Heads	Tails
Historians have used different	another way is by language groups.
One way is by the environment they lived in	would live in the same way.
Not all tribes in any group	ways of classifying Indian tribes into groups.

2 In what ways could you classify people in your school to help outsiders understand it?

3 What sort of classification might an historian find useful if he or she were studying:
    a the settlement of Indians as they moved south from Beringia in the prehistoric period?
    b a possible connection between geography and lifestyle?

4 What advantage is there in studying Indian tribes from different areas in more detail?

1.4 Differences – The Pueblo Indians

The Pueblo Indians get their name from their **pueblos**, villages of permanent homes built out of stone and sun-dried mud bricks. These buildings often had several floors, which were connected by ladders. The Pueblo Indian lifestyle was different from that of other Indians. There were also differences between the pueblos.

Pueblo Indians believed in living as a group, and making group decisions. Everyone had to obey the rules of the pueblo. There were many rules, covering all parts of life. Family life was very important. Most important of all were religious ceremonies. These stressed living in harmony with nature. The religious ceremonies were mostly held in **kivas**, special round buildings, which were often sunk into the ground and reached by ladders. Big religious ceremonies would be held outside, and led by a man called the **cacique**.

Because they had permanent homes, the Pueblo Indians relied more on farming and less on hunting for their food. They ate beans, corn and squashes, with any wild meat that they could get. They also spent time practising crafts like weaving and making pots.

The pueblos traded with each other, and allowed people to marry into other pueblos. They saw themselves as coming from the same ancestors, but they also saw themselves as different. They had different languages. They had different systems for running their pueblos, and for organizing family groups. When the Spanish came, some pueblos were quickly converted to Spanish ways. Some fought the Spanish. Others, cut off by mountains and rivers, had no contact with them.

A SOURCE

A pueblo known as Cliff Palace at Mesa Verde, Colorado. It was built around 1100 and abandoned in about 1275, perhaps because of drought. This pueblo has over 200 rooms and 23 kivas.

Activities...

1 a What was a kiva?
  b How many kivas can you see in Sources A and B?
  c Is it fair to say the Pueblo Indians were religious people? Explain your answer.

2 Why do you think group decisions and keeping to the rules were very important to Pueblo Indians?

3 Why do you think Pueblo Bonito had large and small kivas?

4 Study Sources A and B.
  a Is this how you imagined American Indians lived?
  b Why do you think this is?

Pueblo Bonito in Chaco Canyon, New Mexico. Chaco Canyon is 16 km long. Between 900 and 1200 there were eight large pueblos there. Archaeologists estimate that 200,000 logs were used in these buildings, and that they were all brought in from 40 km away. The people who lived in Chaco Canyon, the Anasazi, also built dams and canals to irrigate their land. The Canyon pueblos were linked to at least 75 other settlements by 650 km of roads. Pueblo Bonito was the largest of the pueblos. It covered more than 3 acres, was five storeys high, and was home to over 1,000 people. It had many small kivas and two great ones, 12 and 18 m in diameter, which could hold hundreds of people.

2.1 Contact!

History suggests that when a technologically advanced society first makes contact with a less advanced one, that contact leads to the slow collapse of the less advanced society. This is what happened in America following Spanish, French and English settlement. This section looks at the first contact between Indians and settlers from England.

The first contact must have been a great shock. The Indians knew nothing of other races across the sea. Their whole view of the world was challenged on the day in 1584 when the English ships arrived at Roanoke Island, in what is now North Carolina. The English attempt to found a colony at Roanoke the next year failed, but they came back to found a successful colony close by within 30 years. More colonies soon followed. Changes were underway that would destroy the way of life of the Indians in this area.

Why didn't the Indians destroy these invaders? Although the English had more powerful weapons, their muskets and swords were not enough to outweigh the Indians' advantage of numbers. Obviously the Indians did not know how it was all going to end. To them, at first, it was an advantage to have the English there.

A SOURCE

The Algonquin Indians fishing with fish traps and spears in shallow water. This was painted by John White, one of the English settlers at Roanoke in 1585.

The English settlers were keen to trade, as were the French in their settlements to the north, and the Spanish in their settlements on the Pacific coast. Usually the Indians wanted to trade as well. They were used to the idea. There had been trade between Indian tribes long before the Whites came.

The Indians were keen to trade because they wanted the goods the Whites had to offer. White people's tools were more effective. Metal cooking pots and fish hooks were highly prized. Even more welcome were guns and knives. With the more powerful tools, Indians caught more when they hunted or fished. With metal pots they could cook food over fire.

This wasn't the only advantage from trade. It changed the balance of power between Indian tribes. Tribes closest to the Whites tried to **monopolize** the trade (keep it all for themselves). Then they made a profit by trading the goods on to other tribes at more than they paid for them. By making sure they kept most for themselves, particularly weapons, they stayed stronger than their neighbours.

Activities...

1 a Study Source A. What advantages might metal fish hooks have given the Algonquin Indians?

b Explain three other advantages Indians might have gained from trading with the Whites.

2 Copy the Beaver Trap diagram.

a Give your copy a key with different shades for **causes** and **consequences.** Shade in your diagram.

b How does this diagram help to explain the changes that contact with the Whites caused?

3 Make your own cause and effect diagram to explain why the Indians didn't destroy the Whites as soon as they appeared.

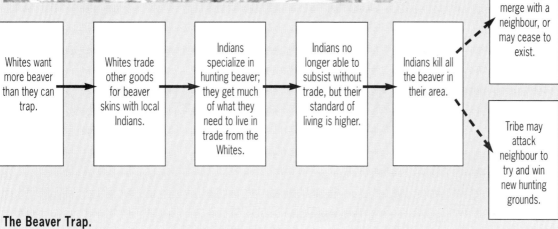

| Whites want more beaver than they can trap. | → | Whites trade other goods for beaver skins with local Indians. | → | Indians specialize in hunting beaver; they get much of what they need to live in trade from the Whites. | → | Indians no longer able to subsist without trade, but their standard of living is higher. | → | Indians kill all the beaver in their area. | → | Tribe may merge with a neighbour, or may cease to exist. / Tribe may attack neighbour to try and win new hunting grounds. |

The Beaver Trap.

2.2 The English Come to Roanoke

In 1584 the English sent an expedition to Virginia, to see if it was possible to set up a colony there. The expedition landed safely, and made friends with the Algonquin Indians on the island of Roanoke. They decided that it would make a good colony and went back to England, with two Indians, to get together a group of settlers.

The second expedition left England in 1585. Thomas Hariot, who had learnt the Algonquin language from the two Indians, went with instructions to find out about Indian customs. John White, an artist, went with instructions to draw detailed pictures of the way that the Indians lived. Most of what we know about the way that the Algonquin Indians lived comes from these two men. Although the English called the land they settled in Virginia, in honour of Queen Elizabeth I (who was known as 'the Virgin Queen'), Roanoke is in modern North Carolina, not modern Virginia.

The Indian village of Pomeiock, painted by John White in 1585.

A SOURCE

B SOURCE

Some towns are surrounded by poles stuck into the ground. They are not very strong. The entrance is very narrow. Only the lord and his nobles have houses in there. On one side is the temple. On the other side is the king's house. Some towns are not enclosed. The houses are scattered here and there. They have gardens to grow tobacco, woods full of deer, and fields to grow corn. They have a special house to bury kings and princes in. These people are free of greed and live happily together.

Written by Thomas Hariot on his return from Virginia.

Activities...

1. **a** List the similarities and differences between Sources A and B.
    b List the similarities and differences between Sources B and C.
    c Do the written source and the pictures mostly agree or disagree?

2. How reliable do you think these sources are as descriptions of Indian life? Explain the reasons for your answer.

3. What were the main features of Algonquin villages?

Their rype corne

Their greene corne.

Corne newly sprong.

Their sitting at meate.

The place of solemne prayer.

The howse wherin the Tombe of their Herounds standeth.

SECOTON

A Ceremony in their prayers with strange jestuns and songs dansing abowt posts carued on the topps lyke mens faces.

The Indian village of Secoton, by John White.

2.3 The Religion of the Algonquin

The Algonquin Indians were very religious. They had temples where the **priests** prayed to their gods. They thought the priests could work magic. They also had **conjurers** to predict the future. We do not know much about their ceremonies, or how much the ordinary people joined in with the religious rituals.

One of the most important jobs of the priests was to prepare the bodies of the kings once they had died. The bodies were skinned, keeping the skin whole. All the flesh and organs were taken out and wrapped, to be stored separately. Then the skeletons were covered with leather, which was stretched over the bones like flesh. After this the skins were put back on. They were left on a high platform, in a separate building, watched over all the time by a priest.

B SOURCE

The priests are old, and seem to be clever men. They shave their hair except for a crest on the tops of their heads and a piece that hangs over their foreheads. They wear a short cloak made of hares' skin, hair on the outside. The rest of their body is naked. They can work powerful magic. They enjoy hunting.

Written by Thomas Hariot on his return from Virginia.

A SOURCE

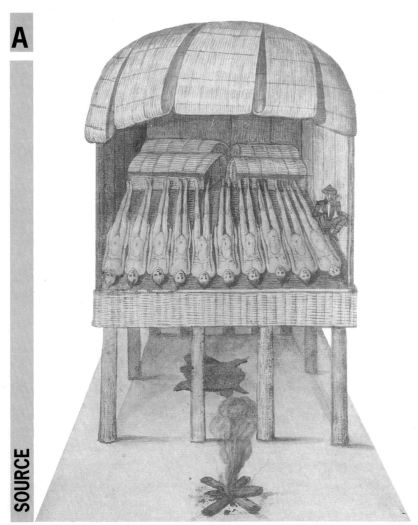

John White's painting of the tomb of the Algonquin kings.

C SOURCE

The people of this country have an idol which they call Kiwasa; it is carved of wood in length four foot. The face is of a flesh colour, the chest is white. The rest is all black, but the thighs are spotted with white. There are white and copper beads around its neck. They sometimes have two or three of these idols in their churches, never more than three. They place them in dark corners to look terrible.

Written by Thomas Hariot on his return from Virginia.

They have conjurers who use strange gestures, and who speak with devils and ask them what their enemies are doing, and other such things. They shave their heads, but for one piece, which they fix a small black bird to, to show what they do. The inhabitants believe what they say, for it mostly comes true.

Written by Thomas Hariot on his return from Virginia.

A painting by John White.

Activities...

1 a Study Sources A and C. What is the figure on the right-hand side of the tomb?

b Why do you think the Indians went to all this trouble with the bodies of their kings?

2 Read Source C.

a Draw a picture of the idol as exactly as you can. What things do you need to know that the source has not told you?

b How might you find out?

3 Study Sources B, D and E. Is the man in Source E a priest or a conjurer? Explain your answer.

4 Describe the main features of the Algonquin religion.

2.4 The English are Going

The first expedition to Virginia, in 1584, was a small one. As far as we can tell, the Indians and the English got on well. We know that two Indians were willing to go back to England. The second expedition, in 1585, was well equipped. The English took things to give as gifts. Hariot had learned Algonquin. The Indians who had gone to England returned with them, to make contact with other tribes. Orders were given not to harm the Indians. It seemed as though they had the firm intention of settling peacefully. Yet they also took 107 soldiers, led by Ralph Lane. Lane was recalled from the war in Ireland. The soldiers outnumbered the other passengers.

The expedition was led by Sir Richard Grenville, a brave man, but not a diplomatic one. Their first landing was on the mainland, south of Roanoke. They were well received in several Indian villages including Secoton and Pomeiock. John White sketched both these villages. Then there was trouble. An Indian was accused of stealing a silver cup. Grenville ordered the Indian's village and its surrounding fields of crops to be burned.

The settlers moved on. Next they landed at Roanoke. Their first move was to build a fort. Grenville returned to England for supplies. Lane and his soldiers treated the Indians badly, and often took their crops. Eventually the chief would not give them any more food. Then the chief led an attack against the settlers. He and some of his men were killed. Relations with the Indians became worse. There were very few English that the Indians trusted. When Sir Francis Drake called at Roanoke to bring supplies, the settlers were so fed up that they all left with him. They were in such a hurry to go that they abandoned three men who had gone on an expedition inland with some Indians.

A SOURCE

Landing was very difficult. We came to a good big island whose inhabitants, as soon as they saw us, cried out in fear, for they had never seen people that looked or dressed like us before. They ran away, howling like wild beasts or men driven out of their wits. But we called them gently back, and offered them glasses, knives, dolls and other things that we thought pleased them. They welcomed us, and took us to the island called Roanoke.

Written by Thomas Hariot on his return from Virginia.

B SOURCE

The wife of an Indian chief and her daughter, painted by John White.

C **SOURCE**

The English met the chief of that place, Wingina, and said that they had heard the place called Wingandacoa. Raleigh later pointed out that this was not in fact the name of the place, but the local way of saying 'you wear good clothes'.

From 'Discovering the New World' edited by Michael Alexander, 1976. Raleigh was taught the Algonquin language by the two Indians who returned to England with Captain Arthur Barlowe. Barlowe was a member of the first expedition to Roanoke in 1584.

D

They are the most gentle, loving, and faithful of people. They are free of all pretence and trickery.

Barlowe writing about the Algonquin Indians.

E **SOURCE**

None shall strike or mistreat any Indian. The punishment will be twenty blows with a club in front of the Indian who was harmed.

Orders given before the second expedition set sail in 1585.

F **SOURCE**

John White's painting of an Indian dressed for war or a feast.

Activities...

1 Study Sources B and F. Describe the way these Indians dressed.

2 What evidence is there that these Indians had been in contact with the English? (Source A might give you a clue.)

3 a Read Source D. What was Barlowe's view of the Indians?
 b Read Source C. How good do you think Barlowe's understanding of the Indians was?

4 Is Source E reliable evidence about how the English settlers treated the Indians?

5 The English attempt to start a colony at Roanoke failed. Do you think this is what the Indians wanted? Give reasons for your answer.

6 Use all the sources in Units 2.1 – 2.4 to answer these questions.
 a What can you say about the level of technology of the Algonquin Indians in the 1580s when the English came?
 b Describe the way the Algonquin society was organized. Was there a social class system? Who ran things?
 c How good a standard of living did the Algonquins have?
 d What feature do all the sources you have used to answer this question have in common?

3.1 Problems of Evidence

The Indians of the North West Coast did not have a written language. They handed down their history, culture and education in their stories, their ceremonies and their art. All these give us a picture of a people living close to nature, the animal world and the world of spirits. They do not give us a detailed picture of the history of these people.

These Indians lived for most of the time in one place. They spent three or four months each year at their summer fishing grounds. They spent the rest of the time in their permanent villages. They lived in large, wooden, communal houses. This should mean that they have left traces of their way of life down the centuries. However, this is not so.

Climate and trees

The Indians of the North West Coast lived on a narrow band of land between the mountains and the sea. The climate is mild and has a rainfall of about 250 cm a year. The mountains rise steeply from the long inlets of the sea; it is easier to travel by canoe than over land. There are dense forests of cedar and other trees on the hills.

Because there are so many trees, the Indians used wood for everything, from building their houses and totem poles to making their cooking boxes, canoes and helmets. In the damp, mild climate things rot quickly. Over the last 100 years wooden houses, horn spoons, buckskin shirts and basket fish traps have completely rotted away. There is nothing left for the archaeologist to find.

B SOURCE

It was very important to have as interpreter the services of the trader's wife, a Tsimshian woman who had been educated in an English mission school.

From 'The Tlingit Indians – Results of a trip to the North West Coast of America and the Bering Straits in 1881' by Aurel Krause, 1956.

C SOURCE

Growing up in the 1960s, I never saw a harpoon, a lance or a buoy made of the skin of a hair seal. The last whale hunt took place in 1913. My great grandfather, Wilson Parker, was a whaler as were his father and grandfather.

Maria Parker Pascua, a member of the Makah people (Nootka tribe), 1991.

A SOURCE

Old totem pole. Few surviving poles are even as much as 100 years old.

Bias

The accounts of meetings with the Indians by explorers, traders and missionaries are all White people's accounts. Because the Indians did not write, we do not have books by them. The Indians who went to schools run by missionaries learned how to write, but they were also taught to look down on the Indian way of life.

All these things make it difficult to find out how the North West Coast Indians lived.

Archaeology

Archaeologists have found shell heaps which show that people have been eating shellfish (and throwing away the shells) for many hundreds of years. Some heaps are taller than a person; some have been found with the stumps of enormous and long-dead cedar trees growing on the top.

Ozette

In early January 1970 a Pacific storm uncovered an old village at Ozette. It had been abandoned when a mud slide covered it in about 1500. The shell rubbish heaps here go back at least 2,000 years. The cedar houses had been buried. Everything except animal and human remains has been preserved in the mud. Archaeologists from Washington University have been working with the local Makah people (of the Nootka tribe). They have found lances, harpoons, little ornaments, spoons and so on. They all date from before the arrival of White people. We know this because there is no evidence of metal tool working.

D

SOURCE

Excavations at the Nootka village, Ozette.

Activities...

1 Write a sentence describing the climate on the North West Coast of America.

2 a How has the climate affected the evidence of how the Indians lived?
   b How do you think the dead stumps of trees help to date shell heaps?

3 Read Source C.
   a How long ago did the last whale hunt take place?
   b What was Wilson Parker's job?
   c What evidence can you find that he was influenced by White people?
   d How do you know that the writer respects both the White and the Indian ways of life?
   e 'It is very difficult to find out what it was like before White people came to the North West Coast.' What evidence can you find to support this statement?

4 Read Source B.
   a When was the writer travelling in the North West?
   b Why do you think it would be difficult for him to get a clear picture from the interpreter of how Indian people lived?

3.2 Ravens and Wolves

Long ago, according to the Indians, everyone in a village was descended from a single family. The whole family lived in a large wooden house. If the family grew too large, a second house was built.

As the years went by there were wars, some people moved away to find new fishing grounds, some married and moved away. The original family (now very large) was scattered. However, the members did not lose touch with each other. They still belonged to their 'house' or **lineage**. There might be several lineages in one village.

When this happened two or more lineages in a village made up a **clan**. Over the years members of the clan moved away for various reasons. This meant that there were members of a clan living in several different villages. But they still thought of themselves as belonging to one clan. Often they kept a special name or had the same clan crest that they could carve on their houses or totem poles.

North of Vancouver Island, among the Haida, the Tsimshian and the Tlingit, the clans were part of even larger groups called **moieties**. Everyone belonged to a moiety. The moieties varied with the different tribes.

Tribe	Moieties
Tlingit	Raven, Wolf (in some villages there was Eagle as well)
Haida	Raven and Eagle
Tsimshian	Raven, Wolf, Eagle, Gispuwudwada (sometimes translated as Killer Whale)

People thought of themselves as belonging to a particular clan led by a chief in their village. However, a person's moiety was also important. A child's moiety fixed the child's rights to certain things during his or her life. It might fix the right to certain fishing places, to future jobs such as carving or boat-building, to the ownership of certain songs and to heraldic crests. Very importantly, it also decided who he or she could marry.

A SOURCE

To prevent romantic slip-ups, a boy and girl in the same moiety were forbidden to speak to each other, even if they were cousins.

From 'The First Americans' by Robert Claiborne, 1973.

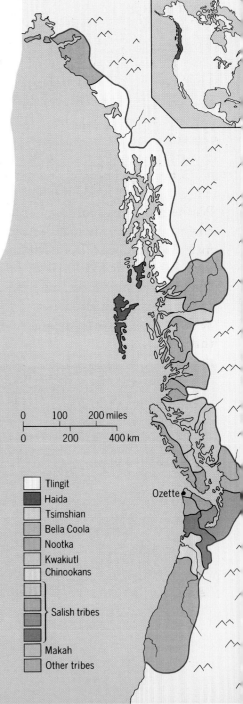

—— Border of North West Coast Indian land

— Main rivers

• Archaeological site

ᴧᴧᴧ Mountains

Tlingit
Haida
Tsimshian
Bella Coola
Nootka
Kwakiutl
Chinookans

⎫
⎬ Salish tribes
⎭

Makah
Other tribes

Ozette

The main tribes of the North West Coast

B *A Haida village squeezed between the forest and the sea. The two nearest totem poles belonged to people of the Raven moiety.*

SOURCE

People could only marry people from other moieties. A Raven could not marry a Raven. A Wolf could not marry a Wolf. For instance, among the Tlingit a Raven woman could marry a Wolf man. Because inheritance passed through the mother, all her children were Ravens.

White people usually divided up the Indians into **tribes**. Often this was based on which language they spoke. This is not how the Indians thought of themselves.

C SOURCE

On the clan crest all Tlingit people had a right to their own moiety. Thus the totem pole of a Raven man would have a Raven carved on it.

From 'Art of the Northern Tlingit' by Aldona Jonaitis, 1989.

D SOURCE

A Haida man of the Raven moiety could marry a Tlingit or Tsimshian woman of the Wolf moiety but not a Raven woman, even though he captured her in warfare. More than this, if a Haida Raven found himself by some accident in a Tlingit village unknown to him, he naturally turned for hospitality and protection to its leading Raven inhabitant. There is some evidence that even in warfare (between tribes), enemies belonging to the same moiety often tried to avoid each other.

From 'The Indians of Canada' by D. Jenness, 1932.

Activities...

1 What was a clan?

2 What were the names of the moieties for the Tlingit clan?

3 a Why was a child's moiety important?
  b Make a list of the things that a child's moiety fixed.

4 How many totem poles in Source B belong to Raven? Give reasons for your answer.

5 You are a member of the Tsimshian tribe. You were born an Eagle. Answer the questions below.
  a What moiety was your mother?
  b You are journeying down the coast in your canoe. Storms blow you off course and you land on the Queen Charlotte Islands where the Haida live. What will you do?
  c The Tsimshian have gone to war with the powerful Tlingit tribe to the north. You are worried that you might kill a member of your own moiety. Is this likely?

3.3 Nobles, Commoners and Slaves

Within their moieties and clans, the Indians had three grades. There were nobles, commoners and slaves. In theory, Indians could only marry their own kind, but in practice some nobles and commoners did marry. Slaves could only marry slaves, if they were allowed to marry at all.

In many tribes, nobles inherited their status through their mother. Nobles were very jealous of their rank within the nobility. A noble man maintained rank by giving **potlatches**. These were huge feasts at which the noble gave away many presents to show his power and wealth.

Some slaves were prisoners of war. Others became slaves through debt. (Once the debt was paid off by working, they were often set free.) Sometimes slaves were kidnapped from neighbouring tribes. Sometimes they were kept or might be sold on. Among the Tlingit, up to one-third of the population were slaves. Most of them were bought from further south. These slaves paddled the canoes, hunted and fished for their masters and did all the drudgery around the village. A chief's wife might have two or three women slaves constantly looking after her.

At a potlatch ceremony, if the host wanted to show he was so rich he cared nothing for his property, he might kill one of his slaves. For instance, he might have one killed to make a roller for bringing his guest's canoe up the beach. Or he might have a slave crushed to death beneath a new totem pole as it was pulled up into place.

B SOURCE

Several neighbouring Kwakiutl tribes moved into Fort Rupert when the Hudson's Bay Company post was established there. Once the tribes occupied a common site, close to the trading post, they were faced with a very acute problem. Each tribe had its own ranking of nobles – one, two, three and so on. This meant that at a potlatch there might be several number one nobles from different tribes. Who was to be the chief guest and receive most presents?

From 'Indians of the North West Coast' by Philip Drucker, 1955.

C SOURCE

An old Indian told me that to say there were nobles, commoners and slaves was a way of simplifying the set-up in order to explain it to the White man. In fact, every single person, apart from slaves, was in his own class by himself.

From 'The Indians of Canada' by D. Jenness, 1932.

A SOURCE

*A wooden hat. On top of the hat is a carving of a beaver. On top of the beaver are **potlatch rings**. A man had one ring for each potlatch he gave.*

Commoners could also give potlatches (this was more usual in some tribes than others). This became more common after trade with White people led to greater wealth among the Indians. They sold furs and fish. Many commoners became rich and could afford to give great potlatches. They gained in status but they did not become noble.

The leader of the village was the **Number One Chief**. He was the most powerful clan chief in that village. Usually the chief's job was hereditary. In the north it was inherited through the mother. Thus among the Tsimshian, Haida and Tlingit, the chief's heir was his sister's son. Further south, the Coast Salish chiefs inherited from father to eldest son. Many of the southern tribes were less rigid about inheritance. Sometimes they would choose the best man from among the old chief's relatives. Among the great whaling people of Vancouver Island – the Nootka – a chief had to prove himself a leader or his people would change loyalty to a better man.

Activities...

1 **a** How many grades of people were there in Indian society?
b What were the grades?

2 Which source disagrees with the gradings for the Indian tribes?

3 **a** Which men in Source D have given potlatches? How many have they given?
b Why do you think men wore hats with potlatch rings?

4 'The Indians of the North West Coast of America had a very complicated society.' Do you agree? Give reasons for your answer.

D

Guests at a potlatch ceremony in 1904.

SOURCE

3.4 Family Life

A man bought his wife from her parents' family. With the wife came privileges that the children would inherit, such as fishing grounds and a clan crest that could be carved on a totem pole.

Once they were living together the man and woman divided up the tasks they had to do. The man did the fishing and the hunting. At home he would make most of the tools and do all of the carpentry. This could be a wooden house, wooden dishes and ladles and wooden chests for storing things in – everything from water and fish oil to masks and capes for dancing at potlatches.

The women collected firewood from the forest and the beach. They gathered berries and shellfish. Often they brought home the animals that the men had killed. Then they prepared the food and tanned the skins to make clothes. They also wove blankets, made baskets and looked after the children.

As children grew up they were taught the things adults needed to know. The girls learnt domestic skills. From the age of ten boys usually went to live with their uncles. They were expected to be very tough.

A modern picture and its caption from 'The Native Americans', Salamander Books, 1991.

Kwakiutl Basket Making, 1850.
A woman and her granddaughter sit working in front of a Kwakiutl village. A dugout canoe has been lifted up (at right) and fish dry on racks below. The house fronts of planks with painted designs, and the totem poles (including one with a moveable beak at the door), resemble those in the village of Alert Bay. Both people show skulls intentionally shaped, the results of pressure in infancy from bundles such as those on the baby whose cradle is rocked by the woman's toe. The woman and her granddaughter have robes twined from cedar inner bark and edged with sea-otter fur. The bark strips for weaving the baskets are kept flexible in water in the wooden box.

Nobody could do just what he or she wanted. Villages were small and everyone knew everyone else and what they were doing. Disapproval by everyone else in the village was one way of making sure people behaved. There were also laws about crimes like murder. The punishment for murder depended on the rank of the victim. A person of the same rank in the murderer's clan had to be killed. Often the person killed was not the murderer.

A 19th century print of the inside of a Nootka house showing the family totem emblems in the background and fish hanging from racks to dry.

Activities...

1 a Write a list of the jobs the wife did. Write a list of the jobs the husband did.
   b Write a list of the jobs a woman might do nowadays. Write a list of the jobs a man might do nowadays. (Remember to list jobs in the home as well as those outside.)
   c What similarities are there?
   d What differences are there?
   e Explain two of the differences and two of the similarities.

2 Sources A and B show different tribes. What similarities are there in clothes and way of life?

3 Source A has two captions – its caption from the book it was drawn for, and a caption in this book.
   a What is the difference between them?
   b Why might historians need the information from both captions?

4 Source A is a secondary source and Source B is a primary source. Does this mean Source B **must** be more useful than Source A?

B

SOURCE

3.5 Religion

The Indians of the North West Coast were very aware of the blessings nature had given them. Animals, the Indians believed, lived to give food to people. However, every animal had an immortal, wilful spirit that might bring disaster rather than riches if it wished. Therefore many religious practices took the form of keeping in favour with the animal kingdom.

Once a year the salmon began to swim from the sea up river to spawn. They came in their thousands in this yearly salmon run. The Indians were thankful that the salmon came to feed them. The first catch of fish was celebrated with speeches thanking and praising the salmon. The fish were treated like guests at a potlatch, for the Indians believed that if they were offended they would not return next year. The bones of all fish catches were returned to the sea. Most tribes would not throw bones to dogs in case the dead animal was offended. If the fish were offended, they believed, they would not allow themselves to be caught again.

Whale hunters of the Nootka tribe took great care to prepare themselves for the whale hunt. They bathed, fasted and spent time in a special shrine praying to the spirit of the whales. The Indians felt that supernatural powers were all around them. A person was particularly likely to be open to the spirits during adolescence. In many tribes boys, and sometimes girls too, went off to live alone for several months. It was hoped they would have visions and acquire a guardian spirit to help them through life. (Unlike most other things, a guardian spirit could not be inherited.)

B SOURCE

The Makah (a Nootka group) knew their lives depended on the Great Spirit Above and they prayed in secret at sunrise. Each had their own way of praying, of finding a spirit helper.

Helen Peterson, a Makah Elder, writing in 1991.

Members of a Kwakiutl secret society photographed in the early 20th century.

A SOURCE

28

C

Some people belonging to the Decitan family captured a small beaver, and, as it was cunning and very clean, they kept it as a pet. By and by, however, although it was well cared for, it took offence at something and began to compose songs. Afterwards one of the beaver's masters went through the woods to a certain salmon creek and found two salmon-spear handles, beautifully worked, standing at the foot of a big tree. He carried these home, and, as soon as they were brought into the house, the beaver said, 'That is my work'. Then something was said that offended it again. Upon this the beaver began to sing just like a human being and surprised the people very much. While it was singing it seized a spear and threw it straight through its master's chest, killing him instantly. Then it threw its tail down upon the ground and the earth on which that house stood dropped in. They found out afterwards that the beaver had been digging out the earth under the camp so as to make a great hollow. It is from this story that the Decitan claim the beaver and have the beaver hat. They also have songs composed by the beaver.

A Tlingit story in 'American Indian Design and Decoration' by Le Roy H. Appleton, 1971.

The spirit world was close by in winter when the Indians had plenty of time. There were many secret societies connected with religion. During the winter, in some places, they took over the village and became more important than the clan. There were very strong secret societies among the Kwakiutl and southern tribes. Often only the upper classes could belong. They put on elaborate shows. They dressed up as the spirits that they worshipped. The ordinary people believed that they were really seeing the spirits. This is not surprising since the society members wore fantastic costumes and masks of feathers, wood, hair, rushes and fur. Many of the masks had moving parts, such as snapping jaws that were secretly manipulated by strings.

These secret societies tended to be a way of controlling the ordinary people rather than a way of encouraging a religious way of life.

Activities...

1 Why did the Indians not throw bones to their dogs?

2 Which sources are primary sources about Indian religion before the coming of the White people?

3 Which sources make it plain that animals were very important to the North West Coast Indians?

4 Which source makes it clear that animals could be very wilful and bring disaster?

5 What do the sources tell us about the Indians' attitude to religion?

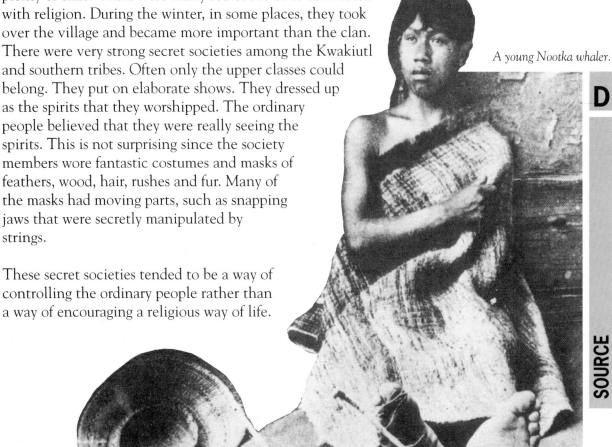

A young Nootka whaler.

D

3.6 Shamans

There were times when Indians fell ill. Then they looked to the **shaman** to help them. Indians believed the shaman could heal both their bodies and spirits. The Indians did not think there were great boundaries between the body and the spirit. In the southern tribes most shaman were women. In the north most were men.

There were many ceremonies held to cure people. The Salish people who lived along the Puget Sound held Spirit Canoe ceremonies. Shamans, who had special powers to communicate with spirit helpers, acted out a canoe voyage into the world below the earth where the souls of the dead stayed. The ceremony caused spirit helpers of the shaman to make the journey to bring back the soul of the sick person. Carved boards and figures were used to help bridge the gap between human beings and spirits. Because they were very powerful and special they were hidden away when not in use.

B SOURCE

The interior of the house was lit up by the firelight. The shaman was seated, naked to the waist, performing incantations over a sick child though the child itself was nowhere to be seen. His long hair, left uncut, was streaming behind him. He was shaking his charms, throwing his body into contortions, uttering shrill cries, hissing and groaning, jerking himself in time to the music.

Heywood Seton-Kan, writing during his travels in 1887, quoted in 'Art of the Northern Tlingit' by Aldona Jonaitis, 1989.

A SOURCE

Story of the Killer-Whale Crest

There was a man called Natsilane (the name of a worm that appears on dried salmon). He was continually quarrelling with his wife. He had many brothers-in-law, who became very much ashamed of this discord but had to stay around to protect their sister. One day his brothers-in-law took him to an island far out at sea, named Katseuxti, and talked very kindly to him. But, while he was out of sight upon the island, they left him. Then he began thinking, 'What can I do for myself?' As he sat there he absent-mindedly whittled killer whales out of cottonwood bark, which works easily. The two he had made he put into the water, and as he did so, he shouted aloud as shamans used to do on such occasions. Then he thought they looked as if they were swimming, but, when they came up again, they were nothing but bark. After a while he made two more whales out of alder. He tried to put his clan's spirits into them as was often done by shamans, and, as he put them in, he whistled four times like the spirit, 'Whu, whu, whu, whu.' But they, too, floated up.

Now he tried all kinds of wood – hemlock, red cedar, and others. Finally he tried pieces of yellow cedar, which swam right away in the form of large killer whales. They swam out for a long distance, and, when they came back, again turned into wood. Then he made holes in their dorsal fins, seized one of them with each hand and had the killer whales take him out to sea. He said, 'You see my brothers-in-law travelling about in canoes. You are to upset them.' After he had gone out for some distance between the whales they returned to land and became wood once more. He took them up and put them in a certain place.

The next time he saw his brothers-in-law coming along in their canoes he put his spirits into the water again, and they smashed the canoes and killed those in them. Then Natsilane said to his killer whales, 'You are not to injure human beings any more. You must be kind to them.' After that they were the spirits of canoes, and, if shamans are lucky, they get these spirit canoes. It is through this story that the Daqlawedi clan claim the killer whale crest.

A story of the Tlingit people in 'American Indian Design and Decoration' by Le Roy H. Appleton, 1971.

The number of shamans in a tribe varied. In the 19th century there were between five and ten for every 1,000 people among the Tlingit. As with many jobs, the position of shaman was often inherited through the mother. The tribes of the North West Coast were well organized. The shamans did not become all-powerful as they did in some other cultures. They worked mainly as medicine men and did not become leaders.

Medicine Mask Dance. A painting of a group of Haida Indians by Paul Kane, 1847.

Activities...

1 What was a shaman?

2 Study Source A.
   a What does 'Natsilane' mean?
   b Write down all the things the story tells you about shamans.
   c Write down the different woods that Natsilane used to carve the whales.
   d What did the Daqlawedi claim because of this story?

3 a Read Source B. How does the writer make you feel about the shaman?
   b Do you think the writer is a White person or an Indian?
   c Rewrite the source in such a way that it is neutral in tone.

D

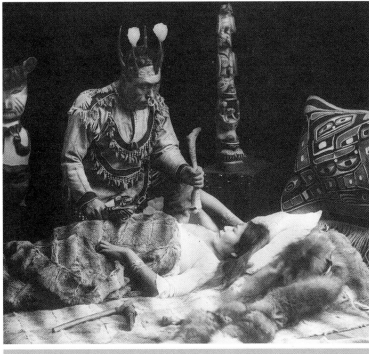

A Tlingit shaman with a sick woman. He holds a shaman's rattle in one hand, and a hollow bone to draw away the sickness.

3.7 Food

SOURCE

A modern reconstruction of a whale hunt. The balloons are sewn-up sealskin floats.

Without the products of farming, most human beings would die in a few weeks. Yet the Indians of the North West Coast lived a comfortable life without learning how to farm at all. The reason for this was the rich fish stocks in the seas and rivers around them.

The Nootka specialized in hunting sea mammals, especially whales. They chased the whales in dugout canoes, often going far from land.

The whale hunt leader inherited his position. Often he had prayed in a special shrine to get a helping spirit. The whale was thought to be too powerful to be caught by human effort alone. The whalers got within 1m of the whale before thrusting their broad harpoons into it. They drove their canoes close to the whale's head to avoid the swipe of the huge tail which could smash a boat to smithereens. A long line (made of whale sinew) was fixed to the head of the harpoon. The men inflated sewn-up seal skins like huge balloons. They tied them to the line. These acted as drags on the whale and marked where it was when it dived. Sometimes a whale would tow a canoe behind it for three or four days before it tired and the men could kill it with long lances. Sometimes a daring man stepped on to the whale's back to thrust in his lance. A respected name among the Nootka was 'Stepping on a Whale'.

B During the summer months, the salmon ascend to this place to spawn. Therefore, all the Indians throughout the surrounding country come to gamble and gormandize for months together. They are very numerous and well disposed; yet they are an indolent and sluggish race, and live exceedingly poor in a very rich country.

SOURCE

From 'Adventures on the Columbia River' by Alexander Ross, 1849.

C The cultivation of potatoes is carried on by the Haida. They give it little attention and produce only small tubers.

From 'The Tlingit Indians – Results of a Trip to the North West Coast of America and the Bering Straits in 1881' by Aurel Krause, 1956.

Other tribes fished the rivers that flowed down to the sea. Every spring salmon swarmed up river to spawn. In some years there were so many that they were pushed on to the banks.

Fish was the basic food for all the tribes on this coast. However, women and children collected berries of all sorts. They were eaten fresh or dried in the sun. There were Saskatoon berries which contain three times as much iron and copper as prunes or raisins; there were cranberries, red elderberries and blueberries. They also gathered seaweed and roots.

The tribes who lived further from the coast, such as the inland Tsimshian, relied on hunting land animals as well as fishing. They hunted mountain goats and bears. The Tsimshian near the sea fished for halibut and cod, seals, sea-lions and sea otters. Many of the tribes valued the oolakan or candle fish which was rich in oil. This was very nutritious. Dried oolakan could also be hung in bunches in the houses and lit like oil lamps.

Most tribes collected clams and other shellfish. This was very important in February, when the winter stores of food were running low and the salmon had yet to arrive.

A late 19th century photograph of a Nootka whaler with a harpoon and seal skin 'balloon'.

Teach your children what we have taught our children: that the earth is their mother. Whatever befalls the earth befalls the sons of earth. If men spit upon the ground, they spit upon themselves. The earth does not belong to man, man belongs to the earth. Where is the thicket? Where is the eagle? Gone. The end of living and the beginning of survival.

From a speech by Chief Seattle of the Squamish tribe in 1851, quoted in 'The Guardian', July 1989.

Activities...

1 List all the foods that were eaten by the Indians.
2 What was their main source of food?
3 a Explain what is happening in Source A.
  b Draw a picture of the whale being chased by the canoe full of men. Use the pictures in this book to help you with the drawing.
4 a Read Source B. What is the writer's opinion of the Indians?
  b Which other sources support Source B?
  c Which sources disagree with Source B?

3.8 Technology

The technology of the Indians was concerned with the things they needed in order to stay alive:

- finding food
- storing food
- making clothing
- making shelters.

They also used their technology in warfare and to make the costumes and carvings for ceremonies.

The Indians were expert fishermen. They used every method known to catch their fish. They speared or clubbed the migrating salmon. They caught fish in nets woven from nettles. They fished with lines of sinew and bone hooks. Several tribes used a type of rake – a wooden pole with bone prongs. The men drew it through a shoal of herring or oolakan and speared several fish at a time. They put woven fish baskets in the rivers as traps. They even made artificial weirs using trees and rocks to narrow the river and make holding pools for the fish. Many skilled people worked together to do this.

For storing food the Indians had discovered how to dry and how to smoke fish. They built special wooden sheds for these jobs.

The hunting of sea mammals such as the sea otter was similar to hunting whales but on a smaller scale. Men needed canoes for hunting and for travelling. They made canoes from cedar trunks. The trunks were hollowed out using an adze or by burning. To curve the sides they used steam. They made steam by putting hot stones in water in the shell of the boat. The Nootka and tribes further south built fairly flat-bottomed canoes with high bows and sterns. This made them more seaworthy.

A **SOURCE**

The free-grained cedar is apt to split with the pounding of the waves. To prevent this, some missionaries have taught the Indians to strengthen the larger boats with ribs but this has failed to meet with general approval.

From 'Up and Down the North Pacific Coast by Canoe and Mission Ship' by T. Crosby, 1914.

Warriors launching a canoe.

B **SOURCE**

A painting by Paul Kane showing a Coast Salish woman weaving a blanket from dog hair and mountain goat wool, another woman spinning the wool, and, in the foreground, a shorn dog.

SOURCE

Carpentry and carving took a long time using stone tools. The men built houses with cedar, split along the grain to make planks. Some tribes used pitched roofs, some used a slightly sloping roof (this made a good platform for dances at potlatches).

The Indians used many baskets, both inside and outside the house. These were woven by the women. Some of the baskets were so closely woven that they were watertight. The women of some tribes also wove cloth. The best examples are the Chilkat blankets of the Tlingit.

D

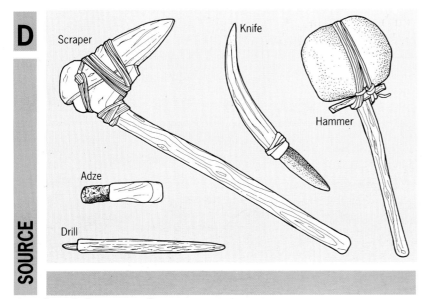

Some basic Indian stone tools.

SOURCE

Activities...

1 a List all the ways you can think of to catch fish.

   b Are there any ways you have thought of that the Indians did not use? What are they?

3 a Draw the tools in Source D.

   b What are the tools made of?

   c What are a carpenter's tools made of nowadays?

4 a Look at Source C. How is the woman weaving combining her work at the loom with her work of looking after children?

   b What did the Indians keep dogs for?

   c What is the woman in the background doing?

5 What evidence is there that the Indians used their technology to wage war?

3.9 Trade and Potlatches

Although the North West Coast Indians lived more settled lives than the nomadic hunters of the Plains, they still moved their villages to their fishing grounds for three or four months in the summer. They did not want to be weighed down with too many heavy possessions. Most trade was in small objects for decoration or immediately useful objects.

Trade was encouraged by **potlatches**. The word potlatch comes from a Nootka word 'patshatl', meaning giving.

People gave potlatches for many different reasons. A nobleman might give a potlatch to celebrate the coming of age of his daughter or son, the building of a new house or the raising of a new totem pole. He might give a small potlatch if he stumbled and fell in front of important people from another village and his own clan. Having made a fool of himself, he would want to show how important he was again. A potlatch might also be given as revenge for an insult from someone of equal rank. The man giving the potlatch showed he was richer and more powerful than the man who insulted him. This also forced the insulter to give a big potlatch in return. Insults could also lead to war.

Although details varied from tribe to tribe up and down the coast, the underlying idea was the same. A man gave a potlatch to gain prestige. He wanted to confirm or improve his rank. In front of all his own clan, his own village and his guests from other villages, he gave away piles of blankets, baskets, furs and chests. The more he gave, the greater he was. Everyone who came to the potlatch was a witness to his success. Sometimes he would destroy his own property like a canoe or kill one of his slaves to show he was so wealthy that these things did not matter. However, he knew that the noblemen who came to his potlatch had to give the same or an even bigger potlatch in return. Then he would be given even more gifts in return for what he had laid out.

Watchman figures wearing potlach rings. Rich men wore one potlach ring on their ceremonial hats for each potlach they gave.

Eagle might be the wife's moiety.

The poles were partially painted: black was obtained from coal and charcoal, red from alder bark or iron ore. Many more colours were used after white people came.

Raven

A potlach was a feast given by a rich man. A moiety is the group a person is born into – Eagle, Raven, Wolf, Killer Whale, etc.

A totem pole of a Raven of the Haida tribe.

The potlatches encouraged both the making of goods and trade. The women wove blankets that might take them months to finish. They also wove capes and baskets. The men made carvings and trapped animals for fur. Sometimes gifts were bought from other tribes. The Chilkat blankets woven by Tlingit women were highly prized. Although potlatches were given by a nobleman, all his clan were involved. They loaned him goods which he then repaid with interest when he was invited to the next potlatch.

When the White people arrived, the sale of furs and fish to them meant that more Indians became rich. More men could afford to give potlatches. The potlatches became larger. More presents were given and more goods were destroyed. Potlatches were forbidden by the Canadian government in 1884 because they were wasteful. Another reason (that was not given to the Indians) was that potlatches were an important way of passing on Indian traditions. Most Whites wanted to destroy the Indian way of life. This law forbidding potlatches remained in force until 1951.

B **SOURCE**

A man of the Raven moiety gave a potlatch to a rival of the Killer Whale moiety. He gave the usual gifts. The Killer Whale man became a drunkard and could not return the gifts as he should have done. So the Raven man carved on his totem pole the figure of a Raven biting the dorsal fin of a Killer Whale. This was a great insult.

From 'Indians of the Americas' by Matthew W. Stirling, 1955.

Activities...

1 What was a potlatch?

2 Following the style of the North West Coast Indians, draw and colour your own totem pole. It should record your own heraldic crest, your moiety, things that your ancestors have done, things that you have done and anything else that you want to put on it.

3.10 Attending a Potlatch

When the day of the potlatch arrived, the important guests appeared. They were dressed in their finest clothes and were greeted by a minor member of the family.

At midday the host and his wife appeared. He would wear a fringed blanket that his wife had probably woven to his own design. She might wear a robe of mink skins. The chief gave a speech welcoming the guests. Then they would go to the feast. This had to be enormous or the chief lost face. His guests sat around and had to eat as much as they could. The rest they took home.

When everyone had eaten well, the chief got to his feet and recited the names, titles and great deeds of his ancestors and his own achievements as a warrior, a hunter and a giver of potlatches. This recital was very important for it was witnessed by his family, clan and guests.

B SOURCE

The potlatch feast consisted of smoked salmon accompanied by bowls of a seal-fat dip; fowl and fresh-water fish roasted on sticks; haunches of venison and bear; bowls of berries – some fresh, some preserved in rancid oolakan fish oil; octopus and halibut boiled in wooden boxes; and as a special delicacy, well-rotted salmon roe and halibut head.

From 'Indians of the North West Coast' by Philip Drucker, 1955.

A SOURCE

Painting of a potlatch ceremony in 1859 by George Whymper.

It was also important that the chief made clear that he was more powerful than his guests. For instance, at a sign a slave might pour a boxful of oolakan fish oil on the fire. The chief would explain that he was worried his guests might be getting cold. As the fire flared up, the nearest guests would have to move back because the flames were too hot. This would give the chief great pleasure. He had forced the other chiefs to move back. That enhanced his prestige.

Finally, the gifts were given out according to the rank of the guests. The potlatch might continue for two or three days with more feasting, religious ceremonies, dances and gift-giving until all the piles of presents were gone. Next year or the year after the chief would travel to another chief's potlatch. He would receive gifts to bring back to his village.

C **SOURCE**

Several of the choicest blankets were handed to the highest ranking guest, together with four robes of sea otter pelts, ten of marten fur and seven of bearskin; the lesser guests divided among themselves the remaining 35 robes of mink and 50 of deerskin. The chief's brother checked the gift-giving process, making sure that the presents handed out to each man corresponded to his rank; a mistake would be considered a serious blunder, to be atoned for only by another face-saving potlatch.

From 'The First Americans' by Robert Claiborne, 1973.

Activities...

1 Use a dictionary to help you find out what the following were: venison; fowl; halibut; salmon roe; marten; mink.

2 Why was the chief's speech very important?

3 Explain why the chief had oolakan oil thrown on the fire.

4 a Have you eaten any of the food mentioned in Source B?

   b If you went to a feast today, what would you have to eat? Mention at least twelve things.

   c What is different about your choice and the Indians' choice? Think of all the differences you can.

D **SOURCE**

A Kwakiutl wedding party arriving for a potlatch, about 1900.

3.11 Art and Life

The people of the North West Coast had a rich culture. Yet there was no farming, pottery or metal working. But they did have a rich food supply and the technology to store food. That meant they could stay in one place for most of the year. They also had leisure time because they had learnt how to store food to eat during the winter. They did not have to keep going out to hunt and fish. They filled their leisure time with ceremonies, secret societies, potlatches, wood carving, basket making and weaving.

There was no dividing line between art and daily life. Artistic objects were also things to be used, such as baskets, hats, boxes, canoes, canoe paddles, horn combs, buckskin shirts and so on. Or they were things of great meaning that could be read as messages, like masks and totem poles.

The Indians had no written language, but many songs and recitals were passed on at ceremonies.

A SOURCE

Nootka basket hat.

B SOURCE

Now I am about to eat,
My face is ghastly pale.
I am about to eat what was
    given me by Cannibal
at the North End of the
    World.

From the song of a member of the Kwakiutl Cannibal Society, quoted in 'The American Heritage' by W. Brandon.

C SOURCE

No matter how hard I try to
    forget you
You always come back to my
    mind.
When you hear me singing
    you may know I am
    weeping for you.

Recorded from the Nootka by a young doctor in the late 19th century.

D SOURCE

There were a brother and sister. The sister had a lover and this made the brother angry. She went away and became the moon. Her brother became the sun. She is constantly trying to keep away from him.

Story quoted in 'The Tlingit Indians – Results of a Trip to the North West Coast of America and the Bering Straits in 1881' by Aurel Krause.

The cult of the Bear appeared among these Indians. One of the secret societies followed the cult of the Bear. The men who belonged to the Bear Secret Society would perform dances and songs, dressed in black bearskins.

They clawed the earth, singing:

How shall we hide from the bear that is moving all around the world?
Let us cover our backs with dirt that the terrible great bear from the north of the world may not find us.

A song could only be sung by its owners, although others might be asked to help perform it. If the owner died before passing on his song, the song died too.

SOURCE **E**

Nootka jewellery.

SOURCE **F**

A carved wooden sun mask, from the Kwakiutl tribe.

Activities...

1 The North West Coast Indians did not paint pictures to hang on their walls. What was their art like?

2 a Which sources make you feel that the Indians were very savage?
b Which sources make you feel they were romantic?
c Which sources make you feel they were scared?
d Which sources make you feel they were artistic and practical?
e Which sources make you feel they were interested in how the universe came into being?
(Answers to these may overlap.)

3.12 First Contact with the Whites

The earliest record of contact between the North West Coast Indians and Whites was in 1741. A Russian explorer, Chirikov, came by ship. In 1774 a Spanish explorer traded with the Haida. In 1778 Captain Cook, the British explorer, arrived.

The Indians were used to trading and were interested in the things the Whites brought. They particularly wanted iron. An iron blade was a far better cutter and carver than stone, bone or teeth. In return they traded furs, particularly sea otter fur. Cook published his journals in 1785. After that, many traders went to the North West Coast to buy furs from the Indians. There was so much hunting that by 1820 the sea otter was almost extinct.

The traders brought guns, but it is not clear whether this meant that more people died in wars between the tribes. The tribes of the North West Coast had always been warlike. The traders also brought alcohol, which had a bad effect on the Indians. The traders did not just bring goods, they brought diseases too. The Indians had no immunity against illnesses such as smallpox. They died in their hundreds.

European claims in 1776. The North West Coast was the last area to be claimed.

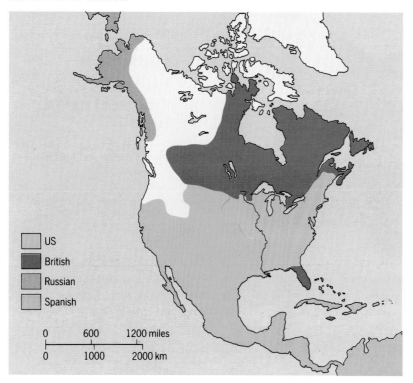

US
British
Russian
Spanish

| 0 | 600 | 1200 miles |
| 0 | 1000 | 2000 km |

A SOURCE

Every man, woman and child carried skins of the otter, the marten, the bear and the beaver. Their relations and friends, they said, were already gone to barter with the people of the coast.

From 'Voyages from Montreal on the River St. Lawrence Through the Continent of North America in 1789 and 1793' by Sir Alexander Mackenzie, 1801.

B SOURCE

The chief became involved in a drinking bout quarrel with a chief of lower rank and stabbed him. The victim's supporters started out with a terrific howling all painted in the most frightening manner and armed with every kind of weapon while the women, possibly even wilder than the warriors, urged them on with wicked cries.

From 'Narrative of a Journey Round the World during the Years 1841–2' by George Simpson, 1847.

C SOURCE

It was common practice on the part of traders in dealing with Indians to use substandard weights and measures. The Indian yard was 35 inches.

From 'The Tlingit Indians – Results of a Trip to the North West Coast of America and the Bering Straits in 1881' by Aurel Krause.

D

Thunderbird totems of a Kwakiutl village, about 1900.

SOURCE

On the brighter side, the trade brought wealth to the Indians. This meant more frequent, better and bigger potlatches. New paints meant that totem poles and masks could be coloured more brightly. Iron meant that more totem poles could be carved more quickly. Canoes were built more easily. The traders did not change the way of life of the Indians. After all, they did not want to. They just wanted the Indians to keep on bringing them furs that they could sell to the rich people of Britain, France, Spain and Russia.

Things did change, however, when the first settlers came. They did not want the Indians. They wanted their land. Some treaties were made with the Indians who were given reservations on which to live. But, treaties or no treaties, the Whites took the land for themselves. Gunboats patrolled along the coast. They were ready to attack Indian villages if they resisted.

Activities...

1 What did the Indians most want to buy from the Whites?

2 What did the Whites want to buy from the Indians?

3 a Read Source A. What is the writer's interest in the Indians?
b What effect would reading Source A have on someone wanting to become rich in 1801?

4 a Read Source B. What is the writer's opinion of the Indians?
b Rewrite Source B as if you were an Indian writer.

5 A group of Indians who traded with some of the Whites wanted to become Christians. They said that any religion that could save the White people must be a good one. What does this tell you about what the Indians thought of some Whites?

6 a Which source supports an Indian view that they were not treated fairly?
b How reliable do you think this source is? Give reasons for your answer.

7 How does Source D show the effect of contact with the Whites?

3.13 The Whites Settle

Christian missionaries came with the settlers. The missionaries wanted to convert the Indians to Christianity and to 'civilize' them. They set up schools for the Indians and tried to teach them how to farm crops and how to keep herds of animals. They saw fishing grounds and land being taken from the Indians and knew that they must be taught another way to live. Unlike most of the settlers, the missionaries really cared about the Indians and wanted them to survive. However, they were very harsh about the Indian way of life; they wanted the Indians to give up all their old ways.

The Indians soon realized that to get jobs in the new fish-canning factories they needed to speak English and have other skills. The mission schools taught them. But they did much more than teach them English. The missionaries and the new White government thought that the Indian way of life was barbaric and heathen. They worked hard to do away with that life.

A

SOURCE

Formerly the Haida had many slaves. Now that war between Indian tribes on the West Coast has almost disappeared under the influence of the Whites, the price of a slave has risen to 200 blankets.

From 'The Tlingit Indians – Results of a Trip to the North West Coast of America and the Bering Straits in 1881' by Aurel Krause, 1956.

B

SOURCE

Interior of a Tlingit chief's house, about 1895.

Potlatches were forbidden by law. This meant that Indian stories and customs could not be passed on to the children. Some children were taken away and sent to mission schools far from their homes. If they were not taken away, parents realized that it did their children no good to live in the Indian way. They were keen for them to fit in to White society.

Along with the fishing grounds, the whaling, the ceremonies and the stories went the art which only had meaning when it was part of a way of life. By the 1930s it looked as if the Indians themselves might become extinct. However, today there is more interest in native Indian rights. Many are asking for compensation for the land they have lost. Indian art and traditions are being revived, but their real way of life has gone.

C **SOURCE**

Our people are ebbing away like a rapidly receding tide that will never return. The White man's God cannot love our people or He would protect them. They seem to be orphans who can look nowhere for help. How then can we be brothers? We are two distinct races with separate origins and separate destinies. Day and night cannot dwell together. The Red Man has ever fled the approach of the White man, as the morning mist flees before the morning sun. However, your proposition seems fair and I think that my people will accept it and will retire to the reservation you offer them. Then we will dwell apart in peace.

From Chief Seattle's speech to the Governor of Washington Territory in 1854.

Activities...

1 a How did the missionaries feel about the Indians?
   b What did Indian children learn at mission schools?

2 a Explain two ways in which the White government stopped the Indians passing on their culture.
   b Did these work?
   c Were there any good things for the Indians about the coming of the Whites?

4 Compare Sources B and D.
   a How can you tell that some men in Source B were rich?
   b Do these sources show the effect of contact with the Whites?

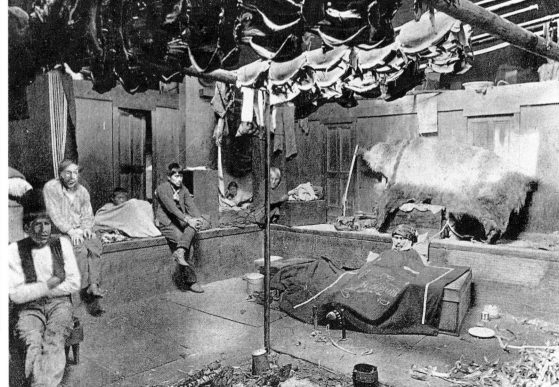

D **SOURCE**

Interior of a Kwakiutl house, late 1890s.

4.1 The Plains Indians

The Sioux was the largest and most powerful tribe on the Plains. They called themselves the **Lakota** (or Dakota or Nakota depending on their dialect), which means 'allies'. Sioux is an abbreviation of an Algonquin word for 'enemy'. There were three main groups of Lakota: the Eastern, the Middle, and the Western or Teton, which is the group we will study. Within the Teton there were important sub-tribes: Oglala, Brule, Sans Arcs, Minnekonjou, Two Kettle, Hunkpapa, and Blackfeet.

At the start of the 19th century the Lakota were nomads. They had little contact with Whites, but their lifestyle had been greatly changed by the horse, first brought to America by the Europeans. For most of the year the sub-tribes, or smaller bands, would wander the plains. Large gatherings of many bands were quite common, especially for religious festivals. Most of the Lakota regarded the **Black Hills** of Dakota as sacred land. This was the area of many of the great gatherings.

A SOURCE

A travois, for carrying the tipi and all other goods from camp to camp. Before they had horses, Plains Indians used dogs to pull the travois.

B SOURCE

The home of the Plains Indian is from 12 to 20 feet in diameter and about 15 feet high. The fire is built in the centre and the smoke escapes through the aperture at the top. It is usually in cold weather too full of smoke to be bearable to anyone but an Indian. The beds are piles of buffalo robes and blankets, spread on the ground close to the outer edge. They serve as sleeping places by night, and seats by day. In this small space are often crowded eight or ten people. Since the cooking, eating, living, and sleeping are all done in the one room, it soon becomes inconceivably filthy.

A description of Indian tipis by Colonel Dodge, an American, in a book written in 1877.

C SOURCE

The tipi is a much better place to live in. Always clean in winter, cool in summer, easy to move. Nobody can be in good health if he does not have all the time fresh air, sunshine, and good water. If the Great Spirit wanted men to stay in one place, he would make the world stand still, but He made it always to change.

Chief Flying Hawk of the Oglala (1852 – 1931).

A Lakota camp, painted by Karl Bodmer in 1833. At the top of the tipi is a cowl which acted as a chimney. It could be shifted according to the wind direction.

E

SOURCE

Some of the tipis were reduced to bare skeletons of poles; the leather coverings of others were flapping in the wind as the squaws pulled them off. One by one the tipis were sinking down, and where the great circle of the village had been only a few moments before, nothing now remained. The covers of the tipis were spread on the ground, together with kettles, stone mallets, great ladles of horn, buffalo robes, and cases of painted hide, filled with dried meat. Squaws bustled about in busy preparation. The horses were patiently standing while the lodge-poles were lashed to their backs. Each warrior sat on the ground, by the decaying embers of his fire, unmoved amid the confusion, holding in his hand the long trailing rope of his horse.

From 'The Oregon Trail' by Francis Parkman, 1847. Parkman was a young White American who spent 1846 travelling in the West. He lived for some weeks with the Lakota band described in this extract.

Activities...

1 Which do you think gives the most reliable description of a tipi, Source B or Source C?

2 a Using all the sources, describe a tipi and a travois.
   b What were their advantages for nomads?

3 What can you say about the different roles of men and women among the Lakota?

4 How might a family like that shown in Source D react if they were offered a modern house instead of their tipi?

4.2 The Buffalo

The buffalo (really a bison, but given the wrong name by early European settlers) wandered the plains in vast herds. It is a large animal. Bull buffalos weigh more than 1 tonne and stand over 1.5 m tall at the shoulders. The cows are smaller, but they were more prized by the Indians because they gave better meat. Buffalos run fast, and have a good sense of smell, but poor eyesight.

The life of the Lakota was based around the buffalo. They were nomads because they moved around the plains following, or looking for, the great herds. Historians have estimated that in 1800 there were about 60 million buffalo on the plains. The Indians lived in balance with the buffalo. They killed plenty, but no more than they needed. Both Indians and buffalo seem to have co-existed without either population rising or falling very dramatically. The Lakota, like all other Plains Indians, used the buffalo to supply most of their needs. They used just about all the buffalo, nothing was wasted. (See the diagram on page 51.)

A SOURCE

At that moment each hunter violently struck his horse. Each horse sprang forward, and, scattering in the charge in order to attack the whole herd at once, we all rushed headlong at the buffalo. We were among them in an instant. Amid the trampling and the yells I could see their dark figures running hither and thither through clouds of dust, and the horsemen darting in pursuit. The uproar and confusion lasted but a moment. The buffalo could be seen scattering, flying all over the plain singly or in groups, while behind them followed the Indians, yelling as they launched arrow after arrow into their sides.

The boys, who had held the spare horses behind the hill, made their appearance and the work of skinning and cutting up began all over the field. The hides and meat were piled upon the horses and the hunters began to leave the ground.

Francis Parkman's description of a buffalo hunt he went on with an Oglala band in 1846.

A buffalo hunt painted by George Catlin, about 1835. Catlin had spent time with Indians on the Plains, and went with them on at least one hunt.

B SOURCE

48

C

SOURCE

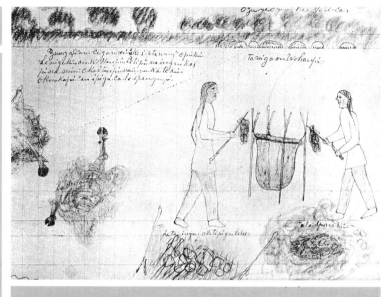

A scouting party cooking buffalo, from Eagle Lance's History of the Oglala. The notes on the drawing, written in Lakotan, say 'cooking with paunch (middle); heating the rocks (left); the cooked meat (right)'.

D

I returned first. In about an hour Kongra-Tonga, with his arms smeared with blood to the elbows, returned. He sat down in his usual seat. His squaw gave him water for washing, set before him a bowl of boiled meat, and, as he was eating, pulled off his bloody moccasins and put fresh ones on his feet. Then he went to sleep.

The squaws unloaded the horses, and vast piles of meat and hides were soon gathered before every tipi. All the squaws and children were gathered around the piles of meat, looking for the best portions. Some they roasted on sticks before the fires, but often they dispensed with this operation. Late into the night the fires were still glowing upon groups of feasters engaged in this savage banquet.

We camped at this spot for five days, during three of which the hunters were at work, and immense quantities of meat and hides were brought in. For the most part, no one was to be seen in the camp but women and children. Still it presented a bustling scene. In all quarters the meat, hung on cords of hide, was drying in the sun. Around the tipis the squaws, young and old, were labouring on the fresh hides stretched on the ground, scraping the hair from one side and the still-adhering flesh from the other, and rubbing into them the brains of the buffalo, in order to make them soft and pliant.

SOURCE

Francis Parkman's description of the Oglala camp after the return of the hunters (see Source A).

Eagle Lance and his history of the Oglala

The Lakota thought history was very important. They had a saying, 'A people without history is like a wind on the buffalo grass'. Their history was usually passed down by word of mouth. Eagle Lance, born in 1869, drew a history of his people in pictures. He started in 1891 and continued working on the pictures until his death in 1913. When his sister died the pictures were buried with her. We only have black and white photos of most of them, taken in the 1930s. They have been used in this section of the book, because they are one of the rare sources to be produced by an Indian, for Indians.

E

After making a fire with the buffalo dung, the Indians put rocks in the fire. Next they took the paunch out of the buffalo, and, after emptying it of its contents, turned it inside out and filled it about two-thirds full of water – it must have held between 15 and 20 gallons. Then they took four bows, fastened them together at the top, and hung the paunch between the bows. As the stones were heated they were put into the water-filled paunch, with the same result as if the water had been placed in a tea-kettle on top of a stove or over the fire. The stones were constantly changed. The meat was put in the boiling water and cooked.

SOURCE

The way a scouting party killed and ate a buffalo. Because they travelled light looking either for buffalo or for enemy tribes, a scouting party would not take metal cooking pots. From 'The Life and Adventures of Frank Grouard', 1894.

F

As soon as the hides were brought in, the women spread them on the ground and pegged them out, flesh side up. Then three or four women would remove all the bits of meat from the hide. In this work they used a flint or piece of sharp stone before steel and iron came into use among them. After all the meat was removed and it (the hide) had dried out, it was turned over with the hair on top. Then, with a tool made of elk-horn, they scraped off all the hair. This tool, clasped in both hands, was used by the women who worked it towards them. When the hair had all been scraped off, it showed a layer of skin which was dark. This was also removed, showing another layer of white. This the women took off carefully as it was used in making a fine soup. The brains and liver were cooked together, and this mixture rubbed all over the skin. It was then folded into a square bundle for four or five days. A frame was now built to stretch the skin. When the skin was opened it was fastened to the frame with rawhide rope. The mixture of brain and liver was now scraped off and the skin washed until perfectly clean. The women then went all over the skin with a sandstone, which made the hide very soft. A braided sinew was then made taut, like a bowstring. The skin was taken off the frame and pulled back and forth on this sinew by the women, until it was very soft.

G

With the skins they build their houses; with the skins they clothe and shoe themselves; from the skins they make rope and also obtain wool. With the sinews they make thread, with which they sew clothes and also their tents. From the bones they shape awls. The dung they use for firewood, since there is no other fuel in the land. The bladders they use as jugs and drinking containers. They sustain themselves on their meat, eating it slightly roasted and heated over the dung. Some they eat raw.

A description of the use of buffalo by the Indians of the Great Plains by Pedro de Casteñeda, a Spanish soldier who was part of a Spanish expedition to inland North America between 1539 and 1541.

Tanning buffalo hides, described by Standing Bear, a Lakota born in the 1870s. He grew up with the tribe, but was sent away to a White-run school in his late teens.

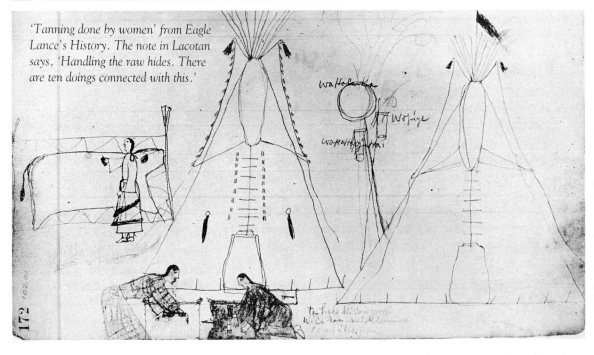

'Tanning done by women' from Eagle Lance's History. The note in Lacotan says, 'Handling the raw hides. There are ten doings connected with this.'

H

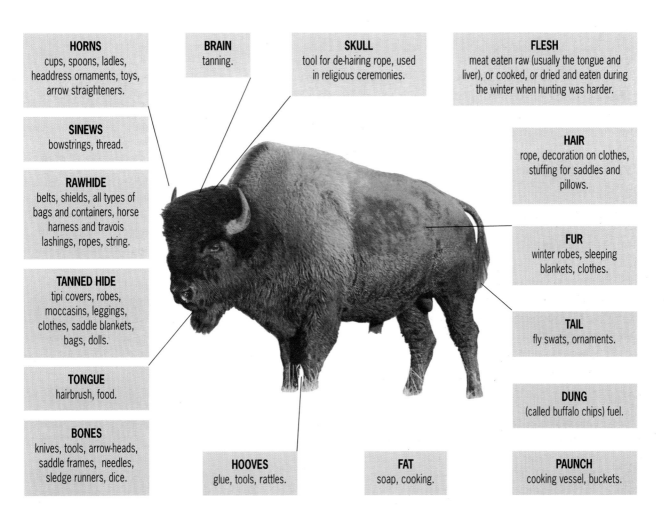

HORNS
cups, spoons, ladles, headdress ornaments, toys, arrow straighteners.

BRAIN
tanning.

SKULL
tool for de-hairing rope, used in religious ceremonies.

FLESH
meat eaten raw (usually the tongue and liver), or cooked, or dried and eaten during the winter when hunting was harder.

SINEWS
bowstrings, thread.

HAIR
rope, decoration on clothes, stuffing for saddles and pillows.

RAWHIDE
belts, shields, all types of bags and containers, horse harness and travois lashings, ropes, string.

TANNED HIDE
tipi covers, robes, moccasins, leggings, clothes, saddle blankets, bags, dolls.

FUR
winter robes, sleeping blankets, clothes.

TAIL
fly swats, ornaments.

TONGUE
hairbrush, food.

DUNG
(called buffalo chips) fuel.

BONES
knives, tools, arrow-heads, saddle frames, needles, sledge runners, dice.

HOOVES
glue, tools, rattles.

FAT
soap, cooking.

PAUNCH
cooking vessel, buckets.

Activities...

1 Does Source B show the hunt described in Source A?

2 Compare Sources C and E.
   a In what ways do they support each other?
   b Do they contradict each other at all?

3 Compare Sources F and H.
   a In what ways do they support each other?
   b Do they contradict each other at all?

4 What part or parts of a buffalo would an Indian use for the following jobs:
   a making bedclothes?
   b making arrows?
   c making a new tipi cover?

5 Source G describes things that happened over 300 years before the other sources. Does this mean there was no change on the Plains in those years?

6 Why might a historian studying the Plains Indians at the time of Source G (about 1540) find Sources C and E useful?

7 Use Sources A and B to describe how buffalo were hunted.

8 Use Sources D, F, and H to describe what was done back at the camp after a kill.

9 What can you say about the different roles of men and women among the Lakota from the evidence in this unit?

4.3 Clothes and Customs

The Lakota had no laws as we understand them. There were many customs which people thought it wrong to break, but there was nobody to make new laws, or to force people to keep the customs. There was usually more than one chief in any band, and chiefs were respected men rather than leaders in our sense. If a chief made a decision, such as to move camp, and some families didn't like it, they simply would not move. Major decisions were debated in a council. In some bands, women were allowed to choose some of the councillors, although the councillors were always men.

Polygamy (men having more than one wife) was normal. There were more women than men, and one hunter could kill enough buffalo to provide food for a number of women and children. Also, tanning hides was a labour-intensive process. The more wives a man had, the more hides he could have tanned. Hides could be traded for goods, such as guns, from the Whites. Another common custom was **exposure**: leaving old people to die when they were no longer strong enough to travel with the band. The band had to travel to find food in order to survive.

B **SOURCE**

They were very fond of their children, whom they spoilt, and never punished, except in extreme cases, when they would throw a bucket of cold water over them. Their children become undutiful and disobedient under this system, which tends to foster that wild idea of liberty and utter intolerance of restraint which lie at the foundation of the Indian character.

Francis Parkman, writing about the Oglala he lived with in 1846.

A **SOURCE**

*An Oglala Council from Eagle Lance's History. His notes say that the four men on the left, and the four men on the right, are **akicita** (officers), and the four in the centre are **councilmen**. Unusually, he added more notes:*
'Rules Established by the Lakota to Govern them in the Past.
1 A number of intelligent men get together and plan or discuss the issue.
2 They select from among the people men of quiet and honest dispositions – four in number – and these are chosen as Councilmen or leaders.
On each side stand two groups of men. These men are officers. They are to guard against any fights or disturbances in camp or on the march. They are four middle aged persons who have done great deeds in battle and who are persons to be avoided.'

C **SOURCE**

A Lakota Chief in full ceremonial dress, painted by Karl Bodmer in 1833.

SOURCE

A group of Oglala women watch part of the Sun Dance through a pine branch fence, from
Eagle Lance's History. This is one of the few pictures to have been photographed in colour.

E

SOURCE

No other race of people has a deeper love of family than the
Sioux. They never punished their children by whipping them or
beating them. Many White people slap their children, snatch
them by the ears, and drag them by the arms, or beat them with
straps and sticks. Indian children were taught respect and
obedience were due to their parents because of the sacrifices they
made. When boys needed discipline they were denied the right to
play war games, practise with bow and arrow, or track an animal
to its den. Girls were denied privileges of playing with their dolls,
helping their mothers prepare a meal around a campfire, or
stitching hardened berries or shells onto clothes.

*From 'The Memoirs of Chief Red Fox',
1971. Red Fox was a Lakota Indian,
born in 1870, who was taken away
from his tribe and sent to a state
boarding school. The 'Memoirs' were
written by a journalist, based on
notebooks written by Red Fox.*

Activities...

1 There was no system of punishments. How does
Eagle Lance's description of the **akicita** help
explain why one might not be needed?

2 Source E says the Lakota had a deep love of
family. The Lakota practised polygamy and
exposure. Does this mean Red Fox was wrong?

3 'Lakota women were second-class citizens.' Does
the evidence in this unit support or deny this
statement?

4 a Describe the clothes of the men and women in
Sources C and D.
   b Do these clothes suggest that the Lakota were
a prosperous people?

5 a Do Sources B and E agree or disagree about
the way the Lakota treated their children?
   b How does this compare with ways of bringing
up children in your area today?

4.4 The Great Spirit

A

SOURCE

Oglala men preparing the ceremonial pipe for a religious ritual, photographed in 1907. A buffalo skull, also used in the ritual, is in front of the men.

The Lakota believed in **Waken Tanka**, the 'Great Spirit'. He arranged the world so that all living things could help and be helped by each other. When they died they could go to be with him in the **afterlife**. Indian life was full of rituals that had to be observed to please Waken Tanka, or the various spirit creatures, or even the spirits of dead people who had not been able to join Waken Tanka.

Sometimes the whole tribe took part in large ceremonies in the ground inside the ring of their tipis. Sometimes religion was a private thing. Part of the initiation ceremony when boys became men was to go off alone, eat and drink nothing and see nobody for several days. At the end of this time they would get a sign from a **spirit animal**. This animal would then guide their lives. They were supposed to keep a sign from this animal in their **medicine bag**. This was a bag that each man wore around his neck. It was entirely private. This was odd, since almost no other part of life was really private in a Lakota camp. The bag was used to keep things that were of special religious importance to that man. When he died, it was buried with him, unopened.

From 'Land of the Spotted Eagle' by Chief Luther Standing Bear, 1933.

B

SOURCE

No good thing can be done by man alone. I first make an offering to the Spirit of the world, that it may help me to be true. See, I fill this sacred pipe with the bark of red willow.

From 'Black Elk Speaks' by J. Neihardt, 1974.

C

SOURCE

The old Indian still sits upon the earth, instead of propping himself up and away from its life-giving forces. For him, to sit or lie upon the ground is to be able to think more deeply and to feel more keenly. He can see more clearly into the mysteries of life and come closer to the other lives around him.

- the pipe
- a buffalo robe
- the heavens
- a red blanket
- shells
- eagle tail feathers
- tobacco
- a sacrifice

A picture of the things which a man needed to pray, from Eagle Lance's History. Behind the Indian is a sweat lodge, used for ritual cleaning.

Two legs share with four legs and the wings of the air and all growing things. Everything an Indian does is a circle and that is because the power of the world works in circles. The sky is round, and I have heard that the earth is like a ball. The winds whirl round, and birds make their nests in circles. Even the seasons form a great circle and come back to where they were. The life of a man is a circle from childhood to childhood. Our tipis are round, like the nests of birds, and they are always set in a circle, the nation's hoop, a nest of many nests, where the Great Spirit meant for us to hatch our children.

From 'Black Elk Speaks' by J. Neihardt, 1974.

They call North American Indians savage, with no religion. I say that they are highly moral and religious beings. I never saw any other people spend so much time worshipping the Great Spirit.

From 'Manners, Customs and Conditions of the North American Indian' by George Catlin, 1844. Catlin travelled with the Lakota and other Plains tribes, before writing his book.

Activities...

1 Study Sources A, B and C. Why do you think these Indians are:
  a sitting on the ground?
  b getting the pipe ready with such care?

2 Study Source D.
  a What items in the list are not in the picture?
  b What items in the picture do not appear on the list?
  c What items in the list can you find in Source A?

3 Read Source E.
  a What reason does the writer give for the Indians camping in a circle?
  b What advantages would camping in a circle have given the Indians?

4 Read Source F.
  a Think about European beliefs. Why might some Europeans have thought that the Indians were savages?
  b Think about Indian beliefs. Why might some Indians have thought that the Europeans were savages?

4.5 Sacred Dances

Some of the Lakota religious ceremonies were for small groups, called **societies**. Each band had several all-male societies that met together under the name of an animal or some other living thing. Other ceremonies were for the whole band, like the **Scalp Dances**, held to celebrate victories after battles or raids. Some of them, like the **Sun Dance**, were for gatherings of many bands.

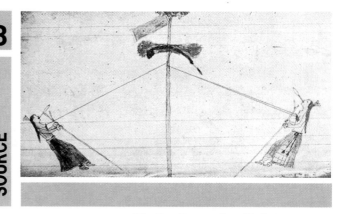

B SOURCE

The Sun Dance, from Eagle Lance's History.

The Lakota prepared for their ceremonies very carefully. They used particular places, particular clothes, and particular decorations for both themselves and the ceremonial pipes. No matter how big or small the ceremony, great care was always paid to the details. Some rituals, like the Scalp Dance, were performed in one day. Others, like the Sun Dance, needed many days of preparation. The warriors would fast, sweat in the sweat lodge, and pray. The ground would have to be carefully prepared. In the case of the Sun Dance there were several days of dances and other rituals before the key part of the ritual.

The Lakota also had smaller rituals that had to be carried out before battle, or hunting the buffalo, or making decisions. There were rituals that had to be carried out to get rid of evil spirits, or bad spells put on you by your enemies. The influence of Waken Tanka was in everything that the Lakota did, and it is not possible to simply divide these rituals into those that were religious and those that were not.

A SOURCE

Indians performing the Elk Dance, from Eagle Lance's History. In this picture of the ceremony, Eagle Lance shows three elk dancers, a medicine man, a man called 'the magic shooter' (who crouches out of sight, supposedly shooting bad magic at the Elk Dancers, which they must dodge), and two women carrying ceremonial pipes. Women did not usually have any part in religious ceremonies. The women here are 'holy women' and were supposed to have magic powers.

SOURCE

C

The Sun Dance from an early photograph.

F

SOURCE

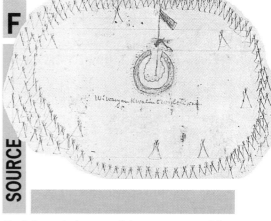

Eagle Lance's drawing of the camp prepared for the Sun Dance. The inside ring is a ring of branches, which make a barricade around the place where the dance takes place.

D

SOURCE

Things needed for the Sun Dance:
A red flannel banner, with offerings of tobacco tied to twigs fixed onto it.
A bag containing a bag with pemmican [dried meat] in it and a bag with red paint in it. Put on the pole.
A buffalo skull, with a blue mark on its forehead, put on the pole.
Two ceremonial pipes.
A blue wooden frame to prop the pipes up.
The hole for the ceremonial pole has to be dug by a man of good habits. Once the pole is in place the ground must be marked into quarters by the priests.

From Eagle Lance's notes to one of his pictures.

E

SOURCE

They had been fasting and purifying themselves in the sweat lodges, and praying. First their bodies were painted by the holy men. Then each lay down under the tree as though he were dead. The holy man cut a place in his back or chest so a strip of rawhide, fastened to the top of the tree, could be pushed through the flesh and tied. The man would get up and dance to the drums, leaning on the rawhide strip as long as he could stand the pain, or until the flesh tore.

From 'Black Elk Speaks' by J. Neihardt, 1974.

Activities...

1 Study Source A.
  a What shape are the tipis laid out in? Why?
  b Copy the picture. Label the ceremonial pipes; the holy women, the 'magic shooter' and the medicine man.

2 Study Sources B and C.
  a Make a list of the things that are the same in both pictures.
  b Make a list of the things that are different.
  c Do the differences mean that someone is doing the dance wrong?

3 Compare Source D with Sources B and C. What are the things on the list that you cannot see in the pictures? Why not?

4 Copy Source F. Label the dance area, the barricade, the buffalo and bag.

4.6 War

War was a constant feature of life on the Plains. The Lakota and the Crow were traditional enemies, and there was fighting between them most years. They did not fight to capture land from the enemy, nor to conquer them. Their aims were to steal horses, to increase their own reputation, and sometimes to get revenge.

Horses were vital in hunting and war. Horses were also the main measure of wealth. To get a good wife, a man would need to own many horses, some of which might be given to the woman's father. Stealing the enemy's horses left the enemy weaker, made it harder for the enemy to retaliate, and made the warriors who stole them much richer. One of the bravest things a warrior could do was to creep into the enemy's camp at night, steal a horse or two, and leave undetected.

Horse-stealing increased a warrior's reputation, but not as much as **counting coup**. To count coup, a warrior had to touch one of the enemy in battle. This was usually done with the hand, or with special sticks and lances. The aim was not to kill or injure the enemy, but to show that the warrior had been in a dangerous place by touching him. Touching a dead enemy was also regarded as counting coup. Killing an enemy was good for a warrior's reputation, but killing was not a necessary part of war.

The Plains Indians believed it was brave to steal horses, to ambush a lone enemy and murder him, or to count coup, but it was not brave to stand and fight to the death if things looked bad. Getting killed was stupid and should be avoided if at all possible. There was no disgrace in running away. One of the reasons Plains Indians tried to avoid being killed in battle was because if they were killed they might be **scalped**. They believed that enemies would continue to be enemies in an afterlife in another world. Someone they killed would be a determined enemy in this afterlife. However, the Indians believed that if a person were scalped, their spirit could not go to the other world. Scalping people they had killed was therefore a way of reducing the number of enemies they would meet in the afterlife. Scalps were also prized as trophies – they showed how brave and successful a warrior was.

A SOURCE

There was a superb head-dress of feathers. Taking this from its case, he put it on and stood before me. He told me that upon it were the feathers of three war-eagles, equal in value to three good horses. He also took up a shield brightly painted and hung with feathers. His quiver was made of the spotted skin of a small panther, from which the tail and claws were still allowed to hang.

Francis Parkman describing the weapons of one of the Oglala band he lived with in 1846.

B SOURCE

During his life, he boasted to me, he had killed 14 men. He told me tale after tale, true or false. Once with a war-party he found two Snake Indians hunting. They shot one of them with arrows and chased the other until they surrounded him. Kongra-Tonga himself seized him by the arm. Two of his men ran up and held the Snake fast while he scalped him alive. They then built a fire and, cutting the tendons in their captive's wrists and feet, threw him in and held him down with long poles until he burnt to death.

Francis Parkman reporting a conversation with Kongra-Tonga in 1846.

C SOURCE

A scene from Eagle Lance's History.

D SOURCE

A scene from Eagle Lance's History.

E SOURCE

A scene from Eagle Lance's History. His notes explain that a Lakota war party found two Crow women, one of whom had a child. They killed all three. Eagle Lance named the warriors involved.

F SOURCE

The Scalp Dance from Eagle Lance's History. Women whose men had been killed danced with the enemy scalps. Brave warriors beat the drums.

Activities...

1 a Why was stealing horses seen as a good way to fight a war?

b What was 'counting coup'?

c Why did the Lakota scalp their enemies?

2 Compare Source A with the other sources. Which tells you most about clothes and weapons?

3 a Describe Sources C and D. What do you think is happening in each?

b Do you think Eagle Lance named the men in Source E because he was ashamed or proud of what they did?

4.7 Victory

Early contact between the Lakota and the Whites came as less of a shock than it had been to Indians in the East. The Lakota knew of the Whites; in the 19th century they saw more and more of them. At first it was hunters, then travellers like Parkman, and finally settlers going through their lands to the goldfields on the west coast. They were disturbed by the numbers, and there was some fighting, but at first they did not feel that their way of life was threatened.

In the early 1860s things got worse as the Whites tried to open the **Bozeman Trail**. This was a route to the goldfields of the Rockies which ran through the heart of Lakota lands. In 1866 **Red Cloud**, an Oglala chief, declared war. The US Army built forts to defend the trail, and Red Cloud besieged the forts. Red Cloud won many small victories, the most important when a party of 82 soldiers under Captain Fetterman was cut off and massacred. The US Government realized it could not defend the trail without spending millions of dollars. It offered to talk. Red Cloud refused until the forts were abandoned and all the soldiers had left the area. The Government agreed. The Army left. Red Cloud's men burnt the forts to the ground. In the **Fort Laramie Treaty** which followed, the US Government agreed to a **Great Sioux Reservation** from which all Whites were forever excluded.

The reservation included the **Big Horn Mountains** and the **Black Hills**, land regarded as sacred by the Lakota. However, in 1874 gold was found in the Black Hills and White miners swarmed into the land. The Indians made many attacks and Red Cloud demanded that the government honour the treaty. It refused, first offering to buy the Black Hills, and then sending the Army to defend the miners.

The Army was commanded by General Terry; one of his senior officers was **General Custer**. Custer was determined to appear as the glorious hero of the campaign. With his cavalry he pushed ahead too far into Indian territory. At **Little Big Horn** he found a large camp of the Lakota and Cheyenne Indians. Without waiting for support, he attacked. Accounts of the battle are confused. What is sure is that Custer and all the troops who attacked with him were killed.

A SOURCE

No White person shall be permitted to settle upon any portion of the territory or, without consent of the Indians, pass through the same.

An extract from the Fort Laramie Treaty, 1868.

Sitting Bull was a Hunkpapa chief and medicine man. Born about 1831 he was seen as being guided by the spirits to protect his people. When Red Cloud led his bands onto the reservation after the Fort Laramie Treaty, Sitting Bull refused. In June 1876 he went through the Sun Dance hoping for a vision of the way ahead for the Lakota. His vision was of a great victory.

B

SOURCE

An artist's impression of the Battle of Little Big Horn.

C

SOURCE

An artist's impression of the Battle of Little Big Horn.

Activities...

1 Why should the coming of the Whites have been less of a shock to the Lakota than to the Algonquin (see page 14)?

2 What caused **contact** with the Whites to turn into **conflict**?

3 a Which of Sources B and C was painted by a White, and which by an Indian? Give as many reasons as you can to support your answer.

   b There are no accounts by Whites of what happened at Little Big Horn – they were all killed. No Indian account says Custer was the last soldier alive, but this is the most common picture of the battle. Why might this be?

4 Custer and his men attacked a much stronger group, and did not run away. Would the Indians have thought they were brave?

Crazy Horse was an Oglala chief most respected as a war leader. He played a leading role in the Fetterman massacre. Like Sitting Bull he refused to follow Red Cloud onto the reservation. At Little Big Horn he was the main Indian leader. In 1877 his people were starving and he did enter the reservation. He was soon arrested and killed while trying to escape.

4.8 Defeat

Little Big Horn was a victory, but it did the Lakota little good. The American Government could not be seen to be beaten. It gave the war against the Plains Indians top priority. The great Indian camp on the Big Horn river broke up. Various bands scattered into the hills, where they were eventually cornered and either forced on to the reservation or killed. Sitting Bull led a large band across the border into Canada, hoping for protection from the British.

Within a year of the battle being won, the war was lost. The Black Hills were firmly and permanently in the hands of the Whites. Even Crazy Horse had taken his band on to the reservation, where he had been arrested and killed. There were no significant bands of Lakota left outside the reservations.

The **reservations** were the Government's solution to what to do with the Indians on the Plains. They were tracts of land, usually land that was of no interest to White farmers or miners, which were 'reserved' for the Indians. Here the Indians were given hand-outs of food and expected to become farmers. There was often conflict between the Indians and the **agents** sent by the government to run the reservations. Many agents cheated the Indians. Some Indians felt the Government in Washington knew about this but did not care.

Sitting Bull and his band returned from Canada in 1881. They were settled on the Standing Rock reservation. Sitting Bull himself spent one year touring America and Europe in a 'Wild West Show'. Most of the time, however, he spent quarrelling with the agent on the reservation.

B

SOURCE

It was the fourth day after Christmas in the Year of Our Lord 1890. When the first torn and bleeding bodies were carried into the candlelit church, those who were conscious could see the Christmas greenery. Above the pulpit was strung a crudely lettered banner: PEACE ON EARTH, GOOD WILL TO MEN.

The last words of 'Bury My Heart at Wounded Knee' by Dee Brown, 1971. Brown told the story of the conquest of the west from the Indian point of view.

A

SOURCE

White views of Wounded Knee.

In 1890 Indians throughout the reservations began doing the **Ghost Dance**. This was based on the ideas of a Paiute Indian, Wovoka. He believed that if the Indians kept doing the new dance, the Great Spirit would soon come to earth, bring to life the Indian dead, and restore the animals to the plains. The Indians would then retreat to the hills and a flood would wipe the Whites from the land. Wovoka stressed the need to be peaceful in the dance. The dancers wore a special shirt, which some believed would stop bullets.

Sitting Bull approved of the Ghost Dance, but did not join in. The dances worried the agents, and soldiers were sent to arrest Sitting Bull. They surrounded his cabin on the reservation, and found him asleep. When they took him outside, a group of Ghost Dancers had gathered. One of the dancers protested and fired a shot. The soldiers killed Sitting Bull and fought off the Ghost Dancers.

Another Lakota chief, Big Foot, heard the next day that he was to be arrested. He decided to take his band to Red Cloud's reservation, in the hope that the old chief could protect him. They were stopped by the Army and taken to **Wounded Knee**. The next morning the Army demanded they surrender their weapons. One man refused and, in a scuffle to take his rifle from him, a shot was fired. Immediately the soldiers opened fire on the now disarmed Indians. Some soldiers were killed by the fire of their own artillery. Most of the 350 Indian men, women and children were killed. The last Lakota resistance to White domination of their lands had ended.

Eagle Lance's view of Wounded Knee. His notes say, 'This was worse than the Custer fight. They even killed a great many children.'

Activities...

1 How might Indians have felt about the reservations?

2 a What were the main ideas of the Ghost Dancers?
  b Why do you think these ideas appealed to the Indians?

3 How might the Whites have felt about Wounded Knee?

4 The Whites called Little Big Horn a **massacre** and Wounded Knee a **battle**. The Indians called Little Big Horn the **Custer Fight**, and Wounded Knee a **massacre**. Who do you agree with?

5 Is Dee Brown right to try to write history from one side's point of view?